LAUGHTER BEFORE SLEEP

Selected Books by Robert Pack

Robert Pack

Laughter Before Sleep

THE UNIVERSITY OF CHICAGO PRESS

CHICAGO AND LONDON

ROBERT PACK is the Abernethy Professor of Literature and Cre-
ative Writing Emeritus at Middlebury College and Distinguished
Senior Professor of Humanities at the Honors College of the Uni-
versity of Montana. He is the author of twenty previous books of
poems, most recently of *Still Here, Still Now* (2008), also published
by the University of Chicago Press.

The University of Chicago Press, Chicago 60637
The University of Chicago Press, Ltd., London
© 2011 by The University of Chicago
All rights reserved. Published 2011.
Printed in the United States of America

20 19 18 17 16 15 14 13 12 11   1 2 3 4 5

ISBN-13: 978-0-226-64419-6 (paper)
ISBN-10: 0-226-64419-7 (paper)

*The author and the University of Chicago Press gratefully acknowledge
the support of the Helene and Richard Rubin Foundation toward the
publication of this book.*

Library of Congress Cataloging-in-Publication Data
Pack, Robert, 1929– author.
    Laughter before sleep / Robert Pack
        p. cm.
    Poems.
    ISBN-13: 978-0-226-64419-6 (paperback : alkaline paper)
    ISBN-10: 0-226-64419-7 (paperback : alkaline paper)
    I. Title.
    PS3566.A28L38 2011
    811'.54.DC   2011004774

♾ This paper meets the requirements of ANSI / NISO Z39.48-1992
(Permanence of Paper).

for Marian Howard

Contents

Acknowledgments

"Late Light" and "Now Once Again" first appeared in *First Things*. "Exchanging Names" first appeared in *Academic Issues*. "An Elephant by Aristotle" first appeared in *Montana Professor*. "Blindness" and "November" first appeared in *Poets of the American West*. "Only the Evergreen," "Loon Call Cantata," and "Panegyric for Charles Darwin's Nose" first appeared in *Explorations*. And "Bubbie" and "Power" first appeared in *Post Road*. My thanks to the editors of these publications for their support of my work.

I Seasons

Late Mountain Spring

Mid-May, and still the maples
bear no leaves; only red buds
offer me reassurance that, as always,
leaves, abundant leaves, though late,
will finally emerge, providing shade
as needed respite
from the enervating summer sun.
Birches display only the catkins
that precede their flourishing,
but soon, I know, leaves will appear;
I must not take the lateness
of spring's blossoming to mean
more than a random weather variant
of nature as it's always been,
more than a meaningless delay
of consolation for bleak winter rain.
Yet lately nothing looks
benign to me as once natural change
appeared acceptable;
familiar sights now seem askew:
a break in the uplifted hawk's smooth flight,
dazed looks in grazing mild-eyed deer
as if they suddenly have something urgent
they would ask me to explain.
But no, such unassigned anxiety,
such morbid reading of the scene, surely
is much too personal—this spreading fear
that clings to everything within my view;
except for us, nature is not
more cruel than it's always been.

Am I projecting my late gloom
on some catastrophe
I apprehend as unpreventable?
      This sense of lateness won't allow
relief from thought—the gripping sense
that human time is coming to an end,
that, as predicted from the start,
from Noah on to the Apocalypse, because
of what we are—the rabid hatreds
separating us—our kind is now
about to bring unnatural destruction
on ourselves eons before the fated sun
collapses and explodes.
      I look into the leafless air as if
its blankness were a prophecy,
and I can see the late Bob Pack
bearing our species' natural remorse
in desperate behalf of everyone he loves,
ascending toward another galaxy
whose aged inhabitants reach out
across light years to welcome,
to embrace, to comfort him.

Alive

       I watch smooth aspen leaves
flash green, flutter to silver,
and return to luminescent green
in the slight uplift of
a wavering September breeze;
and I can see—I live, I am aware—
the red-tailed hawk circle and swoop
and rise again and dip and dive—
because, alive, he can delight
in what he is designed to do,
as I delight in watching him.

       This is his living moment
in which my life also is contained;
this is the moment I contain my life
as if I were the willing author
of my own design, as if the hawk's
stark silhouette against smooth sky
were my original idea.

       His circle widens as he swings
out from the scene and vanishes
behind a swirling cloud
then swiftly reappears, and I am whirled
in an astounding vertigo
of my ascending self—
the opposite of when my body
longs for the release of sleep
or clenches grim with grief
for a beloved friend whom I counted on
and who will not return—as if

my groping flesh encompassed only
urges and dependencies.

      Despite my feverish regrets,
despite work still left incomplete,
I'll concentrate on how
reverberating autumn light
proliferates itself
upon reflecting aspen leaves—
the aspen whispering its name—
on how a jolt of wind joins in as if
it knew the satisfaction of intent.

      And now my earth-bound life
composes everything within
the widened circle of my sight—
I swoop, I rise, I dip, I dive;
now I am pure awareness that I am
aware; I live composed now in lush
exultation that I am alive!

Now Once Again

Now once again the glaring moon,
A mirror in the midnight sky,
A single flower in an empty field,
Evokes the expectation that
An ancient truth will be revealed.

Who knows from where such expectations come,
Some source deluded or inspired,
Ancestral intimations that the moon
Conveys the permanence we know as change,
That what we love must vanish soon.

Thus sorrow for each pulsing thing
That crawls or creeps, slithers or strides,
Is given in this passing night to know
From the dark depth of need, or maybe fear;
Sorrow abides because I think it so.

So this is what the moon proclaims
As it has always done, and always will
For those who watch it at the full,
Who hold it in their sight, and, like our blood,
Feel tidal power in its pull.

Wondering

I wonder if I really have free will,
And wonder if I choose my wonderings.
Is wondering like hiking up a hill
With breathlessness so quickened that it brings

The consciousness of breathing into mind
Thus making possible the willed control
Of how I measure out my breath to find
What body offers up for thought, what role

Intention plays in harmonizing who
I can contrive my remade self to be
With undefined desire? I think of you,
Imagining you're thinking now of me

Picturing you reposed beneath a cloud
So low and lushly luminous it frames
Both you and the bright hill that sings aloud
With swallows swooping their melodic names

Above the shimmer of tall swaying trees.
As in a dream a swirling brook appears
That breaks the silence of the hill to ease
My need for choosing and relieve my fears

Of unnamed innermost dark emptiness—
If wondering and choosing are not free.
Where no self was, let there be ringing YES,
As I choose you, and you have chosen me.

Clouds

A dense gray cloud above the mountain peak
Collides with one that's lighter gray;
A surge of wind blows those charged clouds away
So moonlight glistens on the bleak

Expanse of smooth undifferentiated snow
Above the tree line in the thinned-out air;
Palpable absence hovers there
Where even hungry cougars do not go.

The scene reflects my swirling mind
Contriving still to shape, to see
My inner emptiness, the ghost of me
Expressed, made visible. And so I find

White absence is embellished by
The thought that mirrored thought
Reveals my life as clashed clouds caught
In an upsweep of wind. And that is why

I'll let all introspection go—
My April hopes, my August memories—
To watch blank space define the trees,
And moonlight merge with spectral snow.

Warm Air

Mild summer seems not ready to move on;
September, with ripe apples in her arms,
Remembers and remains, and so warm air
Distracts with its voluptuous charms

From the dull sense of my diminishing,
The dwindling light that shades this scene,
Where mornings gone are visible
And mean what absences must mean.

It's wavering October as I write,
Though maybe I won't find a final rhyme
Before November snow obscures the ground
And whiteness fades into uncaring time.

And yet I see September still—rose apples
Covering her breasts, her private place,
As evening's undulating air reveals
Chilled stillness in her changing face.

Only the Evergreen

for Dan Spencer

The only evergreen not always green,
With null November coming on,
The tamarack lets go its needles as I see
October flourish to its sullen end,
As if one season can encompass both
Mortality and immortality
In its unfolding golden blend.
    Green needles brighten
In their languid mellowing:
Yellow turns gold, gold shades to bronze,
Repeated in the rippling lake,
So slowly over dwindling sunlit days
That I can comprehend transfigured trees
Are destined and designed
To go their modulating ways
To barrenness—and thus their going is
Contained within my mind.
    The beauty of these evergreens
In their effulgent letting go,
Preparing for new beauty coming on—
The silence of bare branches
Underneath the silence of submerging snow—
Is such that I can almost let myself forget
How silence deepens to oblivion
Devoid of yellow, gold, or bronze,
Until all going finally is gone.

Late Light

        Late orange light reflected from the lake
Leaps up into the mountain's shade,
And suddenly a crouching wind
Claws at pale, trembling aspen leaves;
A startled elk, foamed water dripping
From his lips, retreats back from the shore,
His wary head held stiffly high
As in an earlier imagining.
        Perhaps this scene may be composed
Of some sharp sliver of a memory
As if I once lived by a lake; maybe a dream
Of languid autumn water darkening,
Of loons lamenting my heart's own lament—
For what? for whom? I can't recall
The real cause of my gloom or what
I thought the startled elk's eyes meant.
        Dissolved in forest shade, the elk
Huddles among hushed fallen leaves, and I
Can see his lurking absence everywhere
My glum mind seeks to look,
And I can listen to the aftermath
Of moaning loon calls intermingling
All across the undulating lake
Along the sprung wind's swirling path.
        And I myself also have vanished
From the rippling shade of aspen leaves,
Except as whirling consciousness,

Like lilting loon calls echoing
Over lake water when the loons depart,
And wind returns to linger just as wind,
And looming mountain peaks merge with blank sky,
And silence settles in my silent heart.

Bird Feeder

The nuthatch and the chickadee
Are not just navigating through;
They know that they can count on me
To keep their feeder filled with food
In swirling snow and stifling heat,
The nuthatch and the chickadee.

Their fluttering expresses me
From twig to twig to feeder perch;
In merriment the chickadee,
The nuthatch upside-down in search
Of sunflower seeds beneath the tree,
Their fluttering expresses me.

The nuthatch and the chickadee
Are minimal survivors who
Still animate my memory;
They are the shimmer in the dew,
The gleam within the shade I see,
The nuthatch and the chickadee.

Helpless

Early October and as if the winter
In Montana is not long enough,
We've had a killing frost that shriveled all
The aspen leaves, the cottonwoods,
Turned the larch needles brown, depriving us
Of all exotic shades of gold—
Such gold as helps to ease our passing
Into bleakness and December cold.
    The wind-chill factor dropped below
Dead zero, thus suggesting—so it seemed
To me in my own seasonal decline—
That human hatreds, our proclivity for war,
Our wastefulness from pole to pole,
Might be in some horrendous sense
No different than the weather,
Equally beyond volition and control.
    I don't think that I've ever felt
So helpless in the face of circumstance:
The brown and desiccated leaves
As unpreventable as pain that we
Inflict upon each other just because
Enraptured worshippers, as odd
As this may sound, hate someone else because
They think their god's more just and loving than
Some other person's just and loving god.
    So how can I prepare myself
For enervating winter yet to come
Without the consolation offered by
Effulgent autumn with its burnished bronze,

Its copper hues, its shades of gold,
Its ruddy shrubs and purple furze?
     It must be I still need the pretence
That the universe is purposely designed
To offer minds the room to choose
Other alternatives than to destroy;
I need to think that autumn colors have
Somehow emerged to be observed
So that all would-be celebrators might
Compose themselves into a chorus of
Harmoniously shared delight.
     But no, fact has it that the needles on
The larches are depressing muddy brown;
The daily news is bad with rumors of
Impending violence to add more blood
To blood already in the darkened ground.
There's nothing I can do or change
But wait until blown loosened snow
Begins to thaw, red buds appear, streams fill,
And I am able to resign myself
To going where the swirling waters go.

Cheerleaders

It is the championship football game
my high school senior year some sixty years
of memories ago: the stands are full,
the cheerleaders, their smooth cheeks flushed—
I am in love with two of them—cartwheel as if
they're able to defy the pull of earth.
    The clock is running out. I've fumbled once;
I've tackled their bull fullback at his knees,
and I see blinking specks before my eyes.
Our quarterback hands off the ball,
and I break free with eighty yards to go;
one tackler bounces off my thigh,
and no one catches me—I score.
    Now skip ahead one year. I have returned
from college to support my team
and woo another cheerleader.
They lose the game and that vexed night
I dream I go back to the locker room
between the halves. "I have returned,"
I tell the coach. "You're just in time," he says;
"we've left your gear exactly where it was,
so suit up and I'll put you in." The quarterback
calls my best play, the end-around,
and once again I break away and score
the touchdown that makes us the champs.
    For a whole year, at monthly intervals,
the dream returns: I go back to the locker room
at halftime with us still behind.
The coach says, "Suit up, Bob"; again

I shake off tacklers, and I score
the winning touchdown as the cheerleaders
wheel wildly in the pulsing sun.
    And then one night—although the dream
begins as usual—leaving the stands
to go back to the locker room, exclaiming
to the coach, "I'm here!" the dream
surprises with an unexpected turn.
"You've graduated, Bob," the coach replies.
I plead that I'm in perfect shape, nothing has changed,
"You need me if you want to win."
"You're crazy, Bob," he says, "surely you know
that you can never play again."
And that rebuke concluded my recurring dream—
no more high-stepping down the field where once
I could elude whoever was pursuing me.
    Now skip beyond the main grit of my life,
marriage and children, deaths of parents, deaths of friends,
into my own declining age, to something that
I have no wisdom to illuminate—
why my triumphant touchdown dream
returned one final time with tacklers
bouncing off my shoulders and my thighs
as I repeat the touchdown that inspires
the cheerleaders to somersaults.
    But then the dream zooms in upon
the scorer's staring face, and I can tell,
though much like mine, his face is not my face.
I don't know who that winning runner is
although I'm happy for him anyway.
    I watch him walk back to the locker room
in mellowing autumnal light,
the sun's declining warmth upon his neck;

I see the whirling cheerleaders as if
exulting in their pleasure to exult,
suspended in their twirls, poised perfectly—
though not for me—yet surely there
for anyone at any time or any place,
in the enclosing purple evening air.

Among the Constellations

Though blind, John Milton still
could hold the constellations
in his memory as if they shone
right there before his eyes:
giant Orion battling the bull Taurus,
Hercules, holding his great bow,
Castor and Pollux, founding twins of Rome—
each star augmented
by its mythic name.
        As if in his containing sleep,
Milton could see them wheel
and disappear across the sky,
according to the seasons, and because
he knew the heavens so well,
he also could imagine hell for us—
the mind, dissatisfied with what it knows
about itself, and envious.
        Though I can recognize the Dipper
with its handle pointing north
to find Polaris, the bright guiding star,
and can locate glimmering Venus
and shield-wielding Mars,
I know that I belong on earth
with trees and flowers, birds and lakes,
with animals that hide and roam
and nest among these fertile hills—
a place with names I can call home.

And yet I look up in the dark
to locate the Big Dipper, and discern
the outline of a bear because
my predecessors could observe
an earthly creature there,
and I, when in a restless mood,
imagine I can see his mate,
fattened with berries and
prepared to hibernate.
        I'm able to identify with what
had been their wondering,
their longing for repose,
as if just warmth around a fire,
sweet harmony of thoughts with body needs,
was all one ever could desire.
        The constellations, patterned just
of disappearing lights, with each
assigned its momentary place,
what I now choose to celebrate,
the laws of nature as they are,
so I can sleep blind Milton's sleep
beneath the setting of a star.

Indian Summer

Some stubborn leaves still cling
to branches still supporting them
as I sit underneath a reaching birch
I planted many years ago.
So what allows those leaves
to be the ones that still hold on?
      I like assisting nature,
though she really doesn't need
much help from me
in improvising a surprise.
My aging orange cat
snuggles his shape into my lap,
which he will only do
when I'm outside—as if
he's eager to assume
all creatures can be equal there.
      A cat's proclivities—now there's
a mystery for me to ponder
since chance has it that I'm in
a pensive melancholy mood,
a mood with an elusive cause
my introspection can't identify.
      And if that's not, I tell myself,
sufficiently mysterious,
I can at least conjecture that
merely October warmth,
merely the unexpected pleasure of
reposing in the ripened sun
brings pleasant melancholy on—
perhaps because this interval,

now flaring with a swirling flurry
of blurred goldfinches,
seems so contained within itself,
so utterly complete
and indestructible, as if,
incredibly, it is suspended
in a season of its own design.

Seasons

No, no, there's nothing after death!
There's no requited love—unhurried kisses
In a willow's shade—no children who
Pluck tulips for their parents' anniversary;
There are no friends to talk with late
Into the reeling night of shooting stars.
But now, right now, first snowflakes fill the sky
And settle on the stones that huddle
In the ice-frothed stream as we stroll by.

In death there are no streams to sit beside,
Watching pink blossoms on an apple tree,
Envisioning ripe fruit to come; in death
We cannot pause to marvel at the sight
Of yellow undulating aspen leaves
Descending in a pool of their reflected light,

When the roiled sun collapses on itself,
In just about five billion years,
And seasons with their transformations end,
Not even leafless branches will remain
To have their silhouettes described; our words
Will long have vanished into nothingness—
No stones, no streams, no trees, no speckled birds.

Indifferent to that minor alteration
In our galaxy—the sun's implosion
On itself—the universe must still
Continue to expand, thin out, until all order,
All design are gone, and absence, not
Just winter stillness, will prevail; and yet,
Despite the blossomless, the fruitless void,
There's no observer to express regret.

I have no winter consolation now
To offer you, no summer comfort to bestow,
Only abiding sorrow that enables us
To hold each other here and press
Against the multiplying void of nothing
Breeding only nothingness.

Oh, swirling sorrow is the medium
In which we dwell—the solace that we take
In sharing grief for everything
Love has to lose; but now we pause
Beside a swelling April stream
With apple blossoms whitening the air,
Or sit beside a mesmerizing fire
With windy snow descending everywhere.

A yawning bear arises from her sleep
And peers out from her tunneled cave
As if into the afterlife, and then,
An autumn hence, her cubs soothed by her warmth,
She shuffles back to sleep again.

Before blank seasonless oblivion
Begins for you and me, for everyone,
We'll count our losses soon to come
That seem so near, that seem so far,
And, like our parents, hand in hand,
We'll wander back to where we are.

Needing to free my mind from thought,
From words that carry me away from now,
My eyes remind me merely to observe—
To watch arched snowdrops push
Their way above the melting snow,
And now again you're here, emerging
From white morning mist, to tell me so.

November

November, with the humming "m"
Mellifluous inside its name,
Meanders with the now-diminished stream;
The once-green tamaracks, transformed,
Have lost their golden needles, and I see
The sweeping mountain vistas
In the morning light have now regained
Their shimmering chilled clarity.
    Now I imagine that a mellow
And mild drowsiness begins to take hold
In the laden rotund bodies
Of the rumbling bears
Who soon will all lie muffled deep
In humid dens, dreaming
Of what bears dream about, perhaps
The welcoming of sleep.
    The meadow wind has dwindled
To a murmuring, a little less
Than any hushed and human sounds
That mingled with the golden trees
I well remember, and a little more
Than what I know will soon remain
Of memory—brown buried leaves beneath
Mute snow heaped on the forest floor.

The year has whitened to a frost
Upon each stiff unmoving branch,
Reminding me again that I must pause
While struggling to remember
To remind myself of what is gone:
The golden needles of the tamaracks,
My dream about the dreaming bears. November,
And I'm almost ready to move on.

II   Cherishing

Grandpa

Astonishing, I whisper to my wary self,
how early memories return
so vividly in these late years!
I see a sliver of sliced orange peel
fallen upon the floor, and I'm a boy
exploring in the woods, discovering
a salamander underneath a log.
I hold the salamander in my outstretched palm
as swaying hemlocks circle round
the flaring point of orange light
before the memory fades out.
        But then another brightening occurs:
I watch my wife prepare her recipe
of spicy chicken soup as evening light
slants through the window frame, and now, behold!
there's Grandma Ida with her ironed apron on,
her gray hair in a bun, her soft arms bare
above the porcelain kitchen sink.
        I murmur to my rapt, attending self:
that's how the present and the past
become a single instant in my mind,
inseparably merged, each echoing
the echo of the other's voice;
my words reverberate within my listening.
"Ida, the soup's like vintage wine," I say.
        My hushed wife looks at me askance;
perhaps she thinks that I am teasing her
for reasons as elusive as the candle

on the table with its rippling flame
that huddles underneath my breath.

    But levity is not my willed intent—
that's just the way the compliment
bursts from my lips, and I begin to tremble
head to foot, aware that Grandpa's voice
has now returned and entered into me,
as if he still were here, still praising Ida
and her spicy soup with sparkling words.

Kosher Bacon for Aunt Pearl

She never tired discussing poetry
And big ideas: free will and miracles,
Justice and suffering, and when she came
One spring to visit us in our first home,
She dazzled us by telling childhood tales
Of Czarist Russia where she lived in fear
Before her family, their lives at stake,
And just in time, were forced to emigrate.
    Because she felt compelled to theorize
About God's presence in the universe,
Despite the earthy pleasure she derived
From jams and jellies and desserts,
I let myself indulge in the light whim
To tease her just a little bit, and so
At breakfast I informed her that
Bacon served at our house was kosher since
It had, at my request, received a blessing from
A rabbi friend of mine, and thus she was
Set free to savor a crisp slice without
Her violating dietary laws.
    No doubt she saw right through my joke,
But she pretended to believe my claim,
Exploiting it for her own purposes:
To let me know she understood my need
For skeptical detachment when it came
To breaking or obeying rules, to test
What humor can be found in piety.
    Years later, widowed, Aunt Pearl was informed
Her worn heart needed a new valve;
The doctors could replace her faulty one

With the same organ taken from
A healthy pig which, she was reassured,
Would substitute for the defective valve
That had sustained her body's happiness
Throughout the fullness of her dwindling years.
    "Can you recite some holy words," she asked,
"To consecrate the organ of the pig
And make it kosher so it can be used
As if it were my own?" "Baruch atah
Adonai eloheinu melech haolam,"
I chanted over her the prayer I'd learned
To celebrate the Hebrews' hurried flight
To freedom from Egyptian servitude.
Pearl's laughter, as the Polish nurse applauded,
Echoed through that antiseptic room.
    After my dad died of a final stroke,
My mom was courted by an eligible man
Whom she'd met years ago; he'd prospered and
Remained in love with her, and though
He was not Jewish, practical Pearl
Advised her sister she should marry him:
"Solving financial problems is enough
To make him Jewish in Jehovah's eyes"
Was her lighthearted blasphemy to cheer
My mourning mother in her numbing gloom.
But she chose not to follow Pearl's advice:
"You break one law," was Mother's reasoning,
"And you invalidate them all."
    In her declining age Pearl suffered from
Leukemia. Her treatment was to have her blood
Replaced at prescribed intervals.
One winter day when I arrived to visit her
In the hushed hospital, she sat
Propped up in bed, her streaked hair held
In an etched silver clasp with wide-winged birds.

Poems from her youth still filled her mind,
Her favorites—the Odes of Keats.
"With beaded bubbles winking at the brim,"
Aunt Pearl declaimed, with emphasis upon
Alliterated "b," her one loose arm
Extended out to welcome me.
"He died too young," she said, "although perhaps
His genius was enough to compensate
For life he wasn't given to enjoy."
"The donor blood you're getting," I replied,
"Must come from some relentless optimist."

For one long moment Pearl looked far away
As if a cloud cast shadows in her eyes.
"If you do not believe in God," she said,
"How do you know if human suffering
Can be redeemed? How can you tell
When happiness that seems to be what one
Might feel just on an ordinary day
Is really some kind of miracle?"

She paused, took in a breath, pinched redness in
The pallor of her cheeks, lay back, and smiled.
"The food is tasteless here!" proclaimed Aunt Pearl,
Certain that I would comprehend her thought
Of worldly appetite could hold us then
Bonded together right there in the harsh
And flickering fluorescent light.
"I need a meal I can enjoy," she said,
"Next time you come to visit me, please bring
Some Danish pastries and a BLT."

Hands

Nature destroys what it creates,
Including me, and yet when I am
Able to block from my mind
My minuscule share of loss,
I can observe the constellations
On a cloudless night and find
The Dipper indicating north
As if contrived to guide me on
A journey through the spangled sky,
The lion and the scorpion suggesting
Where dread likely dangers lie.

   And there's a vista from a cliff I know
That looks out on the colored crests
Of sunset on the pulsing sea as gulls
Swoop out along the dunes; not long ago,
Alone, I was the one,
Bending into a swirl of wind
Within my shadow on the shore,
As witness to oblivion.

   Though I hate death that must,
As undiscriminating nature wills,
Deprive me of my sight,
I can't imagine an alternative
Better designed to make me care
Or make the living want to live
And cherish fragrance in the orchard air.

   Human unkindness causing harm
Still seems avoidable to me;
Pausing to help lies in the realm of choice,

The willingness to will, and hate, I still—
I must believe, is not necessity.
    Though hands cannot perceive the sky
Or feel the throbbing of the tides,
And can't contain the surging wind,
Or speak the language of alarm,
Hands can reach out—even though
Nature's certain sorrows must be told—
To comfort and to calm.
To stroke, to soothe, to touch, to hold.

Power

They're gone, the powers that I once possessed—
Control of lightning bolts and hurricanes;
Old age does that: fatigue, and care, and stress.
Accepting loss, my last strength, still remains.

One summer night when my first son was four,
A storm came up and frightened him from sleep;
I picked him up, since hugs alone could cure
All aches and sorrows in those days and keep

Him safe from harm, carried him to our den,
And sat him snugly in a chair with me.
We watched a streaking lightning bolt break free
Across the range of snow-tipped mountain peaks,

And, shuddering against my shoulder then,
He said to me, "Again, do that again!"

Woodpecker Reprise

Arriving from the prehistoric past,
out from the tangle of a dense pine grove,
its undulating flight of red dips and red glides
propels the pileated woodpecker
to the thick tamarack where I have nailed
a suet block for him to feast upon.
    What a survival team we make
when we pair up our skills, though
his long ancestry has made it all these years
without my help! Still, something new
has come about as I exchange a meal for him
just for the opportunity to watch
the thrusting of his crested head,
in a red blur, into the suet block
that Mother Nature has contrived for him
with me as her convenient medium.
    It seems She has decided that She wants
appreciation for her quirkiest designs—
improvisations and refinements that
inspire more variations still; she wants
approval for her handiwork, and who
can fault such motivation to invent?
    That is where I come in: my consciousness
to praise, admire, and celebrate.
What else in all creation is so special
and unique, something not heretofore
existing in a mute, indifferent universe?
Observing him, I'm also the observer
of myself observing him—my own red passion in
my own reverberating light.

And there he is profoundly present with
his crest of flame in full display,
his yellow eyes that seem illuminated
from within, his features angular, his body
perpendicular and plump, his beak
and sticky ant-retrieving tongue
repeating what no doubt his whir
of thought repeats and is repeated now
in my red apprehending of his glow,
my predecessor, my replenisher.

Woolly Mammoth

Thawing December, with sleek icicles
Reflecting midday sun along the eaves,
Dazzles my sight, and suddenly
A surge of wind sweeps up among
The tilted pines, then hunkers down, and lo!
The windy snow assumes the body
Of a wooly mammoth, kindred
Of the also extinct mastodon.

The shimmer of reflected light
Flares in my eyes, and yet unfazed
I venture in the swirl to wonder
At my wondering, and yes,
The mammoth is still there as once
Ten thousand years ago it was.

I know our hunting ancestors
Killed them all off, despite their immemorial
Magnificence; the giant camel
And the giant sloth, even the awesome tiger
With its saber teeth—all gone,
All hunted to extinction by our kind.

But now we have recovered, clever
As we are, some of a frozen mammoth's
Still surviving DNA—enough perhaps
So that we might insert it in the egg
Of a live elephant which could produce
A creature partly mammoth, partly
Elephant, and patiently with more
Repeated breedings, then restore,
From humankind's lost past, the animals

Our ancestors obliterated from
The habitat they shared with us.
      Yet that redemption still might take
Another twenty, thirty, forty years, and so
Some godlike scientist will have to figure out
A new technique to bring me back if I
Will really get to see a mammoth
With his mighty tusks outstretched to show
The lady mammoths that he is the guy
They'd want to be the father of their kids.
      In that new age of restitution I
Will wake up woozy from my nap
And walk out in the improvising wind
To see the wooly mammoth standing there
Awaiting me, a message in his eyes;
I'll see the icicles along the eaves
Ignited by the sun in rainbow hues,
My son and grandson hand in hand with me,
As if no time had passed at all.

Socrates's Last Words

"Crito, we owe a cock to Asclepius. Make the offering to him
and do not forget."

I've passed the age at which you chose
to face death with serenity as if
the hemlock poison were an elixir—
the means by which you could complete
who you, intrepid questioner, had always been,
and fix yourself in everybody's memory.
Though you imagined in another world
you might converse with Homer or with Hesiod,
on this plain earth your conversation ceased.
That's what death does, and, unlike you,
I do not have an open mind about
an afterlife, nor do I think that humankind
can overcome its instinct to destroy
in search of justice and transcendent truth.
　　Yet here I am responding to you still
as if you have not left us all behind;
I need to reassure you that I do not mean,
despite my hopelessness, to give assent
to numb indifference or that I've lost
my appetite to reach out or to care.
Like you, rebuking ghost, I'll go on doing
what I've always done—teaching the young
to open their distracted minds to what
the soaring intellect conceives as good:
we're able to respect collective laws
above our greed and personal desires;
we're able to embrace the sorrows
that can bind us to each other in shared grief.
　　An obdurate ephebe, however, I remain:
I do not share your sense of open time,

and I do not believe that souls exist
apart from what mere hungry bodies are.
For me, the interval between one wave crest
and the next describes how briefly
we have vexed this planetary stage.
How insignificant we are, and yet
perhaps our caring counts if only
in our counting our outnumbered days.

How sad, dear Socrates, you can't reply.
I need your humor and your irony—
as when you quipped the punishment
for blasphemy, as you were charged,
for someone as austere as you,
critic of bodily indulgences,
should be to freely dine at the Prytaneum
where the Olympic victors feast.

I need your faith in fatherhood—
as if you could be parent to the world
as well as to your mourning sons—
in order to receive and to pass on
your love of justice, your inheritance.
I join them now at the abyss's edge
as if you waited on the other side.

And so I puzzle over your last words:
your wish to offer to Asclepius,
the god of healing arts, repayment of a debt
for prior services with just one cock.
Did you mean to imply that death can cure
the feverish disease that we call life,
or did you intimate in your sly way
the mindless rooster wisely wakes us all
to welcome in another fleeting day?

Washington

He had no children of his own, yet he
Fathered a nation of anointed sons,
Inheritors of tattered liberty,
Now longing to lay down their guns.

His soldiers had no boots, no overcoats
That crucial winter; with their prospects grim,
Remaining there was how they cast their votes;
Faith in his cause would have to bolster him.

He loved to dance a quickened pace,
His ivory determined smile
Transfiguring his chiseled face
Whose inwardness lacked royal guile.

Suspicious Jefferson thought wrongly
That he wanted to be king. Afraid he'd fail
To leave a legacy of lasting unity,
That consecrated rights would not prevail,

He chose retirement, the final good
Of letting go. But who remained to tell
If death then could fulfill his fatherhood?
His enigmatic last words were: "'Tis well."

The Covenant of Sigmund Freud

He moved to London to escape
The spreading Nazi tyranny, to die
The way his body had decreed—
Slow death by cancer of the jaw—
Writing until the very end, but free.
    The little town of Freiberg,
"freedom mountain," where Sigmund was born,
Might well suggest to an interpreter
That fate connected him to Moses who
Received the law upon a mountain top
And would in time become his ideal
Liberator, though ironically
Freud wished to free mankind
From the belief in God Himself,
From what Freud took to be illusion—
The betrayal of false hope.
And yet he loved collecting jokes;
Martin, his son, reported that
His father had "a merry heart."
    Freud's daughter Anna had been summoned
To Gestapo headquarters, but
A worldly miracle occurred: she was released,
And Freud knew then he'd have to emigrate,
Ill though he was, and fearful
Modern weaponry had brought
Civilization to extinction's brink.
    Hitler condemned psychoanalysis—
Freud's revelation of the potency
Inherent in unconscious thought—

As Jewish science, so the deathwish
Of Nazi ideology could not
Be understood as such and recognized
For how irrational it was as jealous
Hatred of the Hebrew father-God.

     Cancer had eaten through Freud's cheek
When his friend Doctor Schur arrived
To ease his pain; he was astonished at
Freud's equanimity, his grace before
Unmerciful reality. Beloved Anna summoned
Ernest Jones, Freud's loyal colleague
And biographer who honored Freud
With brave restraint in giving vent to grief.
Freud waved to Jones to offer both
A greeting and farewell, maintaining
Dignity through resignation, showing
That it is possible to mitigate, if not
To cure, some human suffering—
Though not the curse of Nazi cruelty.

     His last days were endured by staring
From his study, filled with statuettes
Poised in postures of desire,
At his autumnal garden, symbolizing life
Outliving life—if we might thus interpret
Such effulgence of late blossoming
From what we've learned from Freud's own work.

     His death acknowledged and contained
His body's quintessential truth—
Its frailty—chanceful reality laid bare
In its inscrutability, which finally
Revealed Freud's culminating paradox:
We know we cannot know ourselves—so much
Repression and contingency prevails—
Except to say that love brings happiness,

That oddly some things make us laugh,
That work, transcending self, is good.
        Grieving acceptance was Freud's father gift
To be embraced; surviving Anna would
Inscribe it on the tablet of her heart—
As should we all, to celebrate and mourn,
For all to mourn and celebrate.

Only One

Proud gods, like careless Zeus, are all the same—
They're hot for every mortal girl they see;
Romance for them is just a raunchy game
Because they're bored with immortality.

Without real consequences, pleasures cloy;
Divinity is trapped in what's repeatable,
Unlike the limits of mere human joy
That forces time-bound passions to feel full.

Tempted, Odysseus returned to sea,
Fleeing the island of Calypso's lust
To sail home to his true Penelope
As though he could restore the years he lost.

Not so, and yet their singular carved bed
Did offer compensating poignancy;
Though aged, he would not go uncomforted.
And likewise humbled, are my cares set free.

Cherishing

Can I hold tighter to remaining days?
Is there a hidden art of cherishing?
Must I think harder and review the ways
That meditation's innuendos bring

Fresh resonance and meaning to our love
And make old passions shudder in the blood?
Or is it better to think less, remove
From mind the swirling images that could

Revive the past—bowed willows in the rain,
A stroll around a glowing lake at dawn,
The echoed whooping of a sandhill crane,
Bronze browsing deer upon a shaded lawn?

Forgetfulness makes loss less palpable,
And yet obliterating memory,
Unburdening the aching mind of all
Shared longing for what's gone and cannot be

Won't let my cherishing be satisfied
Without the thought that, yes, I am content.
A willow tree, a whooping crane, lake tide
At mellow dawn—reveal what our life meant.

Encounter

I'd just turned twelve—I'm sure that's right—
and I was wandering along the cliffs
that overlook the sea on a small island
where my parents liked to go
on their retreats. I had to walk
through rough grass near the bluff from where
a hundred feet of winding stairs
led down to the deserted beach below
with bleak November coming on.
    A girl sat on an outcropping of rock,
dangling her feet and swinging them in circles
in the windy air, watching the sun
descend in orange and gold radiance
over the ocean's rim. Surprised
by my own forwardness, I asked if she
would mind if I sat next to her to watch
the gathering display of purple clouds
and their reflection in the sea.
    She nodded with a hesitating "yes,"
and in that pause my mind began to whirl;
as I sat down I grabbed her arm so not
to topple from the ledge; a blast of wind
surged up the cliff as if my blood
were rushing to my eyes, but I held on
although my clinging might have caused alarm.
    A dozen fading years elapsed before
I spied her browsing in a library;
I watched as she thumbed through a book
entitled HOW TO CHOOSE, and said that I
admired the author, how he made the case

there's something in us all enabling us
to reinvent ourselves with words.
She turned to me and smiled; I saw
approval in her eyes, and her quick glance
emboldened me to ask if she
would join me for a drink that night.

     Our conversation probed enigmas
of the human will, and I could sense
she was impressed with me until
I spoke of our first meeting on the bluff—
that we had talked together watching how
the sun sank in the sea, lighting dense clouds
that seemed to be devoured by the dark.
But she could not recall that day,
and she assumed—so I assume—
I must have made the story up as if
inventing such a far-fetched tale
revealed some dubious intent of mine.
Not so. Either I'd been mistaken—she
was not the girl I sat with on the cliff—
or it was just too casual an episode
for her to cherish in her memory.

     I turned the conversation back to how
minds know more than they know they know,
but now she seemed drawn back, remote.
Why had my tale of meeting on the cliff—
even if I was wrong—astonished her?
Although it's possible that she was not
the girl with whom I shared the rocky ledge,
some girl somewhere must still remember how
the blazing waves smoothed to a hush.

     When we next met, again by chance,
I took care to avoid the subject of
our first encounter on the windy bluff,
determined we would only talk about

the mystery of how we have to choose
to make a choice—like choosing empathy.
I must admit I made suggestive hints,
hoping to stir her memory, like telling her
I still enjoyed collecting shells
whose colors make me think of them
as sunsets one can hold in one's own hand.
Although my hints eluded her,
we talked on in the pulsing night, but when
I took her home, some vague and ghostly fear
prevented me from kissing her.

     The next day I decided I would fly
back to the island where my family
had rented a log house deep in the woods
the summer my grandmother died, the year
I met her on that misty precipice.
I had to hike through drying grass
to the same spot where we observed the sun
descend as if it knew some secret place
within the sea—a cave beneath a reef
where yellow fish might sleep and dream.

     I'm sure this sounds irrational,
but isn't knowing that one is irrational
as rational as human beings get?
I saw her sitting on that ledge as if,
unchanged, she actually were there, still there,
her hair streaked out in the moist wind,
watching the orange and red sun
descend and disappear, leaving an afterglow
of purple darkening. And once again,
as if the past repeated and remained,
I asked if she would mind if I joined her
to watch the sea, swirling like steady fire,
and in a floating whisper she replied
that she was glad to have my company.

When we next meet, if chance allows,
dare I risk telling her a slender girl,
resembling her, watched from that cliff,
where I, my mind awhirl, gathered my breath
all those forsaken years ago;
would that mean she can't trust me or that I
am fated to mistrust myself, aware
how hard wet wind was blowing in my eyes?
    Whether we shared that ledge or not—must that
be ascertained beyond uncertainty?
So if indeed we meet again, perhaps
she will accept my version of our first
encounter by the sea, its foam aflame
with fleeting light, as my attempt to name
what some voice in me wishes to believe.
    I think it's likely that throughout
the spinning universe red-orange suns
are setting everywhere, repeating
patterns that repeat themselves, so maybe
she'll remember she was there with me
in one of them, chosen to be our own,
that bleak November day on the cliff's edge.

Loon Call Cantata

Loon calls reverberate across the lake;
Mellifluous, their flow evokes a melancholy so
Impersonal, it might be anybody's
Languid mood, including mine, although

I am astonished by my surge of sentiment.
What correspondence of low echoing—
Loon warbling of delineated sound—
And who I am, has potency to bring

To light this loosening detachment from my self
So that I apprehend my thoughts as though
They lilted gleaming in the air, diminishing
Then fading out? Now knowing what I know

Of disappearances, late loon calls drifting
Into memory, so mellow they express
The murmuring of empty space, I marvel at
The mildness of their lifting into nothingness.

I follow the live lushness of these liquid calls,
Though actual sounds no longer linger there,
Until I float in soothing harmony as if
I could as well be disembodied anywhere.

Naming Mountain Wildflowers

for Janet

My guess is that they've blossomed here
for centuries. And there's forefather Adam,
whom I summon now in memory
to honor him because he was the first
to name the flowers and the animals!
Now with the help of books and friends,
I've learned what some are called,
so I elect to share the pleasure
of identifying them for others just
as I have learned their names, my friend, from you.
    I'll start with showy Shooting Stars
suggestive of the stars in the night sky—
and worthy to pledge faithfulness upon—
as if the heavens and the earth are one,
assuringly continuous
as propagating day, reposeful night,
connecting what appears to be apart.
    Then I'll move on to Prairie Crocus
with its yellow center framed
by pallid purple petals tightly wound.
And since I'm thinking yellow-purple thoughts,
let me augment my growing list
with velvety Delphinium,
with trailing Clematis that binds itself
around unshapely fallen branches, logs,
as if, embraced, dead things
can cycle back to life and bloom
through the remembrance of inheritors.

Returning to the theme of yellowness
as in the Pasqueflower in its purple frame,
I'll sound out Buttercup on my pursed lips
whose brilliant yellow can be found replete
amid the wooly, aromatic Sage.
And thus I have an image to describe
the concept of fecundity: Ah Buttercup,
my own cup runneth over with the names
of what I'm able to identify!
    In this beginner's list, my favorite
Is Old Man's Whiskers with its wispy look
of feathery long tufts, reminding me
of me! I am the rapt observer here,
alive this moment in cascading time,
author of the attachment that I feel
in naming their symmetric shapes—like Yellowbell
(just listen hard and you can hear them ring),
and golden-centered Heart-Leaved Arnica,
and Glacier Lily, and tight Lupine buds
that will emerge as bluish-purple cones,
and pink to white to bluish Carpet Phlox,
and densely clustered Creeping Grape,
Wild Strawberry (not yet quite ripe enough
to feast upon), and Lemonweed
(which native women used in tea
to regulate when they gave birth),
prolific Balsamroot whose gaudy
yellow flowers amid gray-green leaves
display themselves as eager to be seen,
sticky Geranium, and Violets—
their blending shades and hues enlarge
a wanderer's most passionate imagining
of what his moment in the light allows.

My cup—it runneth over with delight
as I walk on in wonder at my wondering,
and so I'll praise forefather Adam now
for his annunciations that first bonded him
to the lush bounty of his fruitful world
and showed the rest of us the way,
and I'll give multiplying thanks
(accompanied by—listen!—colored bells)
to every fervent namer who devotedly
will follow me, as, Janet, I have followed you,
to celebrate a world of worded things,
the budding and unfolding of companionship
across all time and separating distances,
the vow of friendship that shared naming brings.

Bubbie

My first raw book of poems had just come out;
Exalted by my words upon a printed page,
I borrowed my stepfather's car
To drive to Brooklyn where I gave a copy
To my uncle Phil, my mother's sister, Pearl,
And grieving Grandmother who had
Moved in with them when Grandpa died
Quite suddenly, though he had not been sick
One single day of his extended life.
The family had been compelled to flee
From Russia to escape the wild pogroms,
The horseback Cossacks charging down the hill
And splintering their windows and their doors.
    Asked to recite some of my poems,
I sat down with them in the dining room
With küchen freshly made by Grandmother,
And I intoned my yearning cadences.
But Grandma couldn't follow them
In the American vernacular, so Uncle Phil
Translated them into the Yiddish
Grandma understood. And when
I read a poem about my father's heart attack
And mother's fear of loneliness,
The tears cascaded down my Bubbie's cheeks
As they applauded me and asked for more.
    Opponent of the Czar, Phil had evaded
The pursuit of the police, crossing the border
Just ahead of them at night, and now
He was reduced to selling women's clothes—
The price of freedom that he had to pay.

Pearl could intone long passages
Of Pushkin deep from childhood memory
And sing old ballads of the working poor.
   Grandma was always in the kitchen,
Wooden stirring spoon in hand,
Concocting the world's lightest matzo balls,
Gefilte fish, and pastries, küchen
For her daughter's appetite for sweets.
   Is this a scene that even long-lived love
Cannot prevent from windy vanishing—
The table with its blue ceramic vase
Of purple flowers all forgotten and
With everybody gone? Yet, Bubbie, here's
Another poem for you, the taste
Of küchen still upon my lips—as if
Your Yiddish heart might still be listening.

III   Lamenting

Melancholy

Others have been here before, finding
In gloom some sensuous retreat in thought
As on this autumn afternoon
A sun shower meanders through,
And I'm reminded that my mother
Is still dead, though my awareness
That she's permanently gone
Is lightened by my picturing of her,
A fleeting smile transfiguring her face.
Though at the age of ninety-nine she's blind,
Only vague shades of light get through.
So clearly can I picture her
That for an instant she seems really here—
Her memory more vivid and more whole
Than the obscure reality of loss
That has no certain image of itself—
Just an abstract idea, hardly believable.
A sun shower meanders through,
Immediate and palpable,
Where I am sitting on my weeded lawn
With nothing more to do than watch
Sleek swallows in their swoops and arcs.
I can recall my mother reprimanding me
The instant I walked in her door
The last time I flew south to visit her
That I had put on weight, and when I asked
How she could possibly know that, she said
She didn't need her eyes to know
I was not eating properly
Or getting enough exercise.

Not long before she died, my mother asked,
As plaintively as if she were my child,
"Do Jews believe that there's an afterlife?
I need to see my sister and my brother
Once again; there are important things
I never got to say to them." "No, Mom,"
I softly answered her, "The Hebrew Bible
Only says that we are gathered to
Our ancestors and that we merge with them;
That's all the comfort we're allowed."

     Stark disappointment caught her breath,
Tightened her lips; her eyelids closed
As if it were her choice then to be blind.
"Maybe what happens after death," she said,
"Depends on what we're able to believe;
Maybe my sister's sitting by a stream—
Do they have streams in paradise?"
Her mouth turned down in worry that
She'll wait in vain for my arrival there
Because I can't pretend that I believe.

     Though I can see my mother still,
Her chestnut eyes, her rounded face,
I have no picture of her being gone;
All I have left to cherish and believe in
Is mild momentary warmth
Of an autumnal shower that in passing
Merges sunlight previously here
With wafted rainy shade now coming on.

Pain

How pure is suffering, how perfectly
Body pain can obliterate
Affronts and jealousies and pangs
Of surging envy; even hate

Dissolves and dissipates when pain
Intensifies—hatred spontaneous
That seems unreal, uncaused,
Or hatred that's inspired in us

By unrequited love, betrayal by
A trusted friend—heartbreak
Made inescapable by passing time.
Red rolling sunsets on a lake,

Shagged trees emerging from the mist
As on the morning of creation day—
Spectacles that we call beautiful—
Pain wipes such visionary sights away.

And who we are becomes anonymous,
Self-realizing work remains undone;
When body has been so usurped
We are the same, we're anyone.

Evacuation

Here's how it happened as I best
remember it. The fire marshal informed us
that the fire was still ten miles away,
but that we would be wise to pack
some basic things, like documents,
mementoes, and computer files,
and be prepared to transport animals—
carrying cages for our cats,
portable kennels for our puzzled dogs—
in case the August wind flared up again
and caused another blast of angry fire
to jump the back-burn area,
too fiercely hot to be contained.
Yet he assured us, we would have
a full day's warning to load up our cars
and move to somewhere safe.

Next dawn, however, knocking at our door
back in the forest where we built the house
our son designed ten years ago, he urged:
"You've got to leave right now, just take
your animals, your photographs,
a change of clothes, prescription medicines,
and get the hell right out of here!"

I took a box of my most treasured books,
copies of Shakespeare's plays with notes
I'd written in the margins over many years
that guided me when teaching those loved plays
of natural evil, natural good—
notes that now marked the changes in the way
I understood the sorrows and the laughter

in the universe, and thereby recognized
the transformations in my aging self.

  As I approached the door to leave,
there stood my wife, her seasoned frying pan
firmly in hand, her floppy velvet hat
askew at a defiant angle warning
spirits of destructive winds and fires
that they had better take heed of her wrath.
She paused a prolonged moment deep
in thought as if perhaps there might be
something else essential she should
gather in her arms, or maybe she surveyed
the memories, attached to souvenirs collected
through the years, like paintings, pottery,
antiques, ceramic animals,
that now would all be lost except
as stories told to grandchildren.

  And, after all, what meaning does life have
beyond the sharing of a tasty meal
with family or friends, beyond the way
we look back or we look ahead
with satisfaction or disgruntlement,
beyond the stories we delight to tell?

  We could not know malicious wind,
like some tormenting stepmother,
would choose then to reverse herself
as if repenting what she'd done,
and that our home would luckily be spared,
the monster mother transformed back
to wind, to fire, to what she always was.

  However windy fire might challenge us
to bring forth consolation from blind nature's
immemorial indifference,
my wife would have her frying pan;
she'd have her destiny-defying hat;

she'd have her vision of what fire
illuminates as precious even if
it ravaged everything we owned.
    And I would have this story to relate,
including for our grandchildren—
safely beside me at our great stone hearth—
suspicions that the fire had been set
by someone wicked hiding in the woods.

Humankind

My father was a senator
at the dark time of Roosevelt's New Deal.
The local district that elected him
(now filled with drug dealers, burned out)
back then was lower middle class,
composed of Irish and Italians and us Jews,
quite typical of the south Bronx.
    I went to Public School 48
while Hitler and the Nazis conquered France;
in that mixed neighborhood I often
had to fight the bullies, older kids,
who taunted me for killing God
as I was walking home from school.
    But I had my own band of friends—
not all were Jews and one was black—
and at election time we put up posters
of my dad and tore down every one
belonging to the guys opposing him,
but Dad softly admonished me
and made me put them all back up.
    How much I still enjoy recalling this,
though over half a century has passed!
How vividly the poster picture of my dad,
his moustache and the deep cleft in his chin,
his smile, lives in my mind.
                    Dad always won
despite the fact that he, against
strong pressure from the Church—the priests
who uninvited called on him one afternoon—
supported legal use of contraception,

which, at the age of ten, I couldn't talk about;
"Children should be wanted," Dad explained.
        The memory that after half a century
remains most lucid in my mind was when,
for company, Dad drove me up to Albany
because the Senate session had begun.
Dad put me in the wire enclosure where
Governor Lehman kept the terriers
he bred and raised, so I could play with puppies
to my heart's content.
                                When I turned twelve,
my dad decided that I needed
an activity more suitable for a young man
almost bar mitzvah age, so he arranged
for me to sit beside the Senate chair
and bang the gavel for the session to commence;
he knew that I'd be good at that.
        By chance, the issue of the day
was a new antivivisection bill, and I,
emboldened with instinctive justice
on my side, asked if I could address
the senators all gathered there.
Here was an issue that I knew about,
clearer than whether contraception
was against the will of God or when
a human soul was born.
                                "Like people,
animals feel pain and want to live!"
I spoke out in my wavering soprano voice.
I still can hear surprised applause among
the suddenly attentive senators,
though that, if you choose to include
our current presence in Iraq,
amounts to five resounding wars ago.

On our way home, though he looked pale
and sadness dimmed his eyes (he died
from a fifth stroke when he was forty-six),
Dad said to me in his most soothing voice:
"Someday, when there is less hostility
toward Jews, you could be president."
    And like a gavel thump I cry out now
in my assertive voice—as if
my father were still listening—
for everyone to hear and heed,
though I'm not president, not even
an aspiring senator, "Do not hurt animals,
whether or not a God looks on,
cause no one harm, be kind to everyone
who can feel pain, be kind, be kind!"

Inheritance

An anti-Semite is a person who hated me before I was born.
—Elie Wiesel

I went to all-male Dartmouth College
More than half a century ago—
That was my father's dying wish—
When the admissions board enforced
A firm restrictive quota on both blacks
And Jews, and there was only one
Fraternity on campus we could join—
As if some law of nature, something written
In one's genes, decreed it to be so
That difference must breed mistrust.
    The starring lineman on the football team
Was nicknamed Butcherhouse; he wore
A fraying T-shirt all the northern winter long,
Displaying his imposing hairy belly in
Defiance of the cold—as if declaring dominance
Meant more to him than staying warm.
    One night he deigned to visit our fraternity
To demonstrate he could outdrink us all,
And we were humbled as we had to be;
We understood the silenced place to which
Deference to his strength assigned to us.
    When I arrived at Middlebury College as
An English prof in 1964, I soon discovered
Not a single Jew was tenured there
Or ever had been tenured in the past.
I was the first, years later, to receive
Such recognition, and my friends anointed me
The Jackie Robinson of academia.
    Back then, the proper thing to do
Was disapprove of prejudice

And yet do nothing else, in toleration of
Intolerance. So when the most outspoken
Campus anti-Semite, Pistol Buck,
Called me a "dirty Jew" in public at
The president's reception on
A sunny graduation afternoon,
I took a swing at him, but was restrained
By friends who wished to keep a truce.
     Ah, yes, we always must be tolerant!
Which one of us would not profess to that?
Who wants more violence and war?
Who wants to wander through the centuries
Protected only by one's wits,
And virtuous—since power corrupts—
By counting on the good will of the powerful?
Is it not possible that virtue might
Turn out to be its own reward right here
On earth, not in some afterlife, and we
Could all belong to one fraternity?
     Was this the reconciliation that my father,
With his final breath, hoped to achieve,
Recalling how his father with his only suit
Escaped resentful Germany right after
World War One but still before the Nazis'
Unimaginable purge began,
To safety and assimilation in America
Where they might warm their working hands
At one collective visionary fire?
     Inheritance—like memories that I
Have lived myself, that's who I am:
The temple sacked, the broken ark,
The desecrated scroll, the banishments
Across the hostile continents,
The lying charges of conspiracy,
The gaping ovens swallowing the weak—

Always the weak, the weaponless,
Who take their virtues with them to
Their uncomplaining, smoky graves.
　　　From somewhere almost hidden on the map
A voice now surges up within my voice:
"Never again!" I whisper to my father in
The shudder of the cringing night.

Blindness

As she approached the age of ninety-nine,
my mother lost her sight—dependency,
the last humiliation that her body
laid on her, threatened her sense
of who she was and how she wished to die.

And yet her other senses were intensified;
although she'd always loved to eat,
now she would chew more slowly,
lick her lips, and savor sweet or sour,
or salty, peppery, tongue-curling tart.
Her facial muscles would relax
and smile lines form beside her sightless eyes.

She'd sit on her apartment balcony
in humid Florida where she had lived
with my despondent stepfather
for forty years, and listen to the waves
pulse on the shore as if in harmony
with her strong, thrumming, stubborn heart
that still resisted letting go.

She needed a maternal caretaker
to supervise her all around the clock,
bathe her, set out her medications,
tuck her snugly into bed at night
and reassure her in the afterlife
she'd be united with her family—
each one exactly as they were.

I'd fly down with my sister when we could
arrange the time to visit her;
leaning on her walker for support,
she'd meet us at the door and tell me

that I'd put on weight. "How can you tell
that I've gained weight?" I'd ask,
if you can't see?" "A mother doesn't
need to see to know when her own son
neglects his health," she'd sternly claim.

  The three of us would sit beside each other
on her woven couch, and she'd inquire about
my sister's kids and mine, and I would ask how she
was managing. She'd place her fingers
on my sister's eyelids, then on mine, pressing down
until our sight went out. Her voice
rehearsed and wavering, she'd say,
"Just think the word 'alone,' and let the sound,
that rolling O, toll slowly in your mind
inside the dark with only you to hear
and only you to know that sound is there—unless,
unless you're able to imagine that
you're with each other, just as I'm with you,
inside that separating dark—a dark
extending further than you've ever gone."

Junerose

Junerose, that really was her name
Despite her black hair and her cream-smooth skin.
She and her mother spent that summer in
A yellow cottage by the lake
From where we rented ours as a retreat
So my sick father could be cared for by
My frantic mother, read his worn books,
And hopefully recuperate.

Junerose worked as a waitress at
The local diner where I saw her first
And learned her father had been shot down
Over Germany, that, at sixteen,
She was just one year older than I was,
And that her fiancé, a college guy,
Had the prized job of lifeguard at our lake.

I organized a party at our house
For all the kids that lived nearby,
And, as luck had it, Junerose came without
Her fiancé and hung out close to me
That humid night on our screened porch,
As Mom insisted, so that we would not
Disturb my failing father's sleep;
Ah, cheek to heated cheek, we danced as fireflies
Wooed each other in the shrubbery.

Toward dawn we wandered to the beach
To watch the looming moon descend behind
The silhouetted hills across the lake.
We strolled along the shore with naked feet
As suddenly a tear slipped down her cheek;
I asked if I'd said something wrong,

Though I had nothing really to confess.
She gazed at me with her green eyes,
Replying only how the silver light
Spread out upon the windless lake.
Those were the very words she spoke.
And then she paused, as if she could
Prolong that moment in the waning night
To tell me that her father swam this lake
Before his country summoned him.

     I did not know if I should take her hand
Or try to kiss her on her lips, although
I understood how deeply moved she was
Just witnessing the misty dawn arrive—
How in a surge the risen sun transformed
The lake into a mirror of hushed trees.

     I let one day go by, and then I called
To ask if she'd go out with me—a movie
Or the carousel at the amusement park—
But she said "no," her lifeguard fiancé
Would not approve her dating anyone.

     I saw her briefly only one more time
As that swift summer dwindled to an end:
One evening, sitting on the beach alone,
I watched her rise up dripping from the lake,
The gleam of water steaming from her arms,
Her black hair shining in the sunset glow,
And yet some hidden fear prevented me
From simply calling out her name.

     I spent that drizzling autumn by myself:
I'd stroll the beach and climb through brambles
To a meadow rough with drying clover heads
With its wide vista of the harbor side
Where her young father kept his motor boat.
I found a gilded leather book,
Abandoned by a circle of charred stones

That marked some couple's campfire site,
But didn't recognize the poems inside.
That was the fall my father died without
Departing words for us. His silence
Made me think of how her father's cry
Went unheard in the roar of his descent.

      And now a half a century's gone by.
I wonder if Junerose is still alive
And married to that lifeguard guy; I wonder
If I passed her on the street or spotted her
Through the reflecting window of a coffee shop,
Would I still recognize her round high cheeks,
The gray-green sorrow in her eyes
That for one moonlit night reached out to me?

      I'm pleased to muse that in the afterlife
I'll be fifteen again because, at heart,
Love does not change—just as my mother said
When my dad died: days follow after days
Like somber dawn repeating in a lake;
Memory outlasts what vanishes.

      So I imagine that I will remain
What I have always been—a boy who searched
For turtles sunning on a drifting log,
Admiring sunfish as they flashed beneath
Lush lily pads: I'll picture Junerose with
Black gleaming hair and moonlit skin,
Grieving for her doomed father as his plane
Streaked downward through the smoke-filled sky.

      A book-bound father now myself, I find
Mild mellow comfort when I speak her words,
Like "silver light" and "windless lake," as if
I hear her voice in mine in whisperings
That help me to recall what Junerose meant:
That's how the past continues on,
"Spending again what is already spent."

Obsolete

A century or so from now
When our reorganized inheritors
Have brains internally computerized,
Containing libraries, how will historians
Consider us—will they regard us
With contempt for our vast ignorance
Since we are merely biological,
Barely evolved, still in a carbon phase,
Or will they care enough to empathize
With our capacity for suffering?
    Suffering by then will no doubt be
Virtually obsolete, only a concept
That pertains to our crude evolutionary phase
Before all body parts and organs
Had become replaceable. And yet perhaps
Our calm inheritors will wonder if they've lost
Something of value, something quite precious
That, along with our defining sense
Of transience and of flux, gave poignancy
To our vicissitudes, almost redeeming them—
Diminishment of appetite with age,
Decay and ordinary accident,
Forgetfulness, delirium,
The house with all its shutters closed,
The last words of the grandmother:
"A family must hold together like
The grip of thumb and fingers on a hand!"
    So maybe our inheritors will wonder
If our intermittent happiness—
A sudden leap of sunlight on a lake

At dawn, the mountains' purple haze
Advancing like a wakening from sleep—
Depended on the certainty of loss:
Entangled in a hooked, protruding branch
Of a sleek floating log, the white
And baffled face of a drowned boy
Who walked among us only yesterday.

      And yet what meaning can a yesterday—
As we record and mourn the past—
Provide for our inheritors?
Will they have any sense of time at all
If they can't measure time by loss?
And yet might one of them, still curious,
Suspend his brain's enhancements so
He can experience what we were like?
Might he not wish to sit beside a lake at dawn
And watch a family of circling ducks,
Their green heads stunningly ablaze
With sudden light, and might he weep
For fleeting pleasure and recover
A lost plenitude in his unbidden tears?

      What would I say to him if he
Could conjure me to sit beside him by
The shimmer of the lake beneath
A willow's murmuring, quick chickadees
Like notes upon the branches of the tree?
How much of my own sorrow would I want
To share with him? Would he resent
Being reminded that he was not present
In that close, reverberating room to hear
My mother scream when Grandma's hand went still?

Tehran, 2009

for Neda Agha-Soltan

The students protest in the swirling streets
under the desiccating sun, waving
hand-printed placards that demand
their votes be counted honestly.
A beautiful young woman, coughing blood,
shot by a sniper from a roof nearby,
lies in her father's baffled arms;
in twenty minutes she'll be dead!
No kinder government will come of this;
weapons alone determine who will rule,
just force, uncomprehending force.

I'm taken by surprise political
concerns can stir compassion in my mind—
as if what happens in this hurtling world
should matter to a person of my age
with human history to dwell upon,
its intermittent music amid violence.
Ahead lurks apprehension for our species—
being what we are, the bombs our genius
has contrived—what our inheritors
are likely destined to endure.

Nothing can ease her father's grief;
the moaning circle of his mouth
howls out for help that will not come.
No thoughts of mine can comfort him;
nothing about her death can be redeemed.

Nor can his grief distract me from my life,
what little there remains of it to spend
with some last purpose yet to be contrived.

I have a vanishing to undergo—
to be betrayed by my conflicted heart.
Is it not vain of me to mourn for her
as if to share her father's agony?
Dawn after dawn, the saga of our woe
goes on repeating what it's always been;
we do not have the fortitude, the will
to alter or transform ourselves.

      Her father holds her sprawling body in
a desperate embrace. Perhaps somehow
he still can squeeze breath back into her lungs;
perhaps some cosmic pity or remorse,
that's waited for its time to enter in,
will make all soldiers drop their guns, appalled
as dark blood bubbles at her lips
where honeyed kisses should have been.

      But I must concentrate on what
remains for me to do: compose my mind
to face oblivion with equanimity,
accepting fleeting nature as it is—
indifferently cruel beyond imagining,
whose doubtful compensation is
that groaning sorrow brings forth sympathy,
the searing tears that generate more tears.

      Gently is her sunken body lifted up
and carried from the public square;
her face is covered by a neighbor's scarf,
embroidered in bright yellows, browns, and reds.
The camera askew, anonymous,
can only focus on her father's back,
hunched down into itself, already
indistinct as uncomplaining earth.

      A brief reprieve to care for someone far away
whom I have never met is all I have—

a moment in blue shade beneath a tree,
out from the unrelenting sun that's blind
to the tormented world it shines upon.
    Oh, what more can I do than squeeze my eyes
and try, as long as I have time, to hold
her lonely beauty steady in my mind
and hear her father's moan as if it were
the solace of an oboe's notes that float
among the whirling spheres and do not know
tomorrow, from today, from long ago.

Enemy

With his thick legs apart,
his bony fingers on his hips, I spy him
            standing with stark sun
behind his head, turning his ears red,
            in the forsaken place
he well might have already left
            if ever he were really there.
And yet I see his raven looks,
            his yellow eyes, his slicked-back hair,
or maybe I recall him from a book
            with dragons and horned beasts.
I do suspect he doesn't like me, though
            his hot hostility might be
impersonal or my imagining:
            what can he really know
about my life, my sorrows, my regrets?
            But if it is not me he hates,
who might I be mistaken for—someone
            he thinks has given him real cause
to seek revenge if only for
            some inadvertent slight?
I am not paranoid or blind—
            I recognize real danger with
my acid sweat when my bones quake
            and my taut sinews cringe.
I know when it's not safe to risk a chance—
            to trust and not protect myself.
When he gets close enough I'll shut my eyes
            and thrust my silent knife

deep in his ribs until his blood is spilled
     to cry out from the ground.
Though I'm not certain he's the one
     I can identify among
the others who resemble him, their ears,
     their eyes, their hair, their teeth,
I'll do what must be done in order to
     outlast him and survive.

Transfigured

The poem of mine that caused the greatest stir
In my recital to an audience
Of college kids is whispered in
A lullaby by a young mother
Half asleep, nursing her infant
On a moonlit night as trees bend in the wind.
        A clear-eyed coed strode up to the podium
To chastise me: I had no license to presume,
She claimed, that I, a male, can understand
Just how a female body can affect
A woman's feelings or her thoughts.
        My blurted-out reply was that I have
A mother and a sister and a wife
And therefore can through observation
And through empathy imagine what
A woman's inmost thoughts might be
As milk flows from her risen breasts—
So that my fatherhood encompasses
Such wide and wonderful imaginings.
        This reasoning offended her,
And she rejected the validity
Of empathy as real experience
Which I claimed counted as a basic part
Of my identity. I was surprised
By her hot vehemence, and noted how
Her cheeks and ears flushed glowing red,
Enhancing, as I must admit,
Her adversarial attractiveness.

So I attempted still another ploy—
Some comedy to lighten our dispute:
Before the male Y-chromosome kicks in,
Pontificated I, all fetuses
Are female, thus the first phase of my life—
Which no doubt I am able to recall
At the unconscious level in my brain—
Is based on existential womanhood
Predating the chagrin of having nipples
Undistinguished even as display,
Merely exaptations, functionless.

To my dismay, that didn't make her laugh;
Was she too young to comprehend
Where my imagining was coming from?
Perhaps the failure to connect was mine—
A failure of the very empathy
That I had boasted of? I felt the sudden urge
To end the confrontation and head off
With local friends to get a drink.

Inspired by my frustration, I composed
A painful look of shocked sincerity,
And, hands clasped, I confessed that years ago
I'd undergone a sex-change operation that
Transformed me from a woman to a man,
Merely a little shift from X to Y,
Although I still contained emotions my
Once female body had aroused in me.

That whopper caught her off her guard!
Though surely she suspected fraudulence,
She didn't dare to challenge me
In case her mistrust might be wrong;
She didn't want to risk intolerance.
I told her she should buy my latest book,
And watched her stride off down the empty aisle.

That balmy night in the hotel, with voices
Echoing along the corridors,
Before at last I fell asleep, moonlight
Repeating in the window squares,
Assuaged by friendship and by beer,
I tried to conjure up her radiance—
A suckling infant circled in her arms—
And me beside her taking it all in.

Falling and Rising

He stood up in the stern of the canoe,
extending his arms out as if he could
embrace the wind, then suddenly
he tumbled backward, disappearing in
the frigid lake. Holding smooth gunwales
for support, I scrambled over
intervening thwarts to reach
where he had vanished from my sight;
I locked my fingers on his whitened hand,
the only part of him that I could see,
but could not pull him up. He sank
as if a whirlpool pulled him down, and I
was stranded at the edge of the canoe
as slant rain battered at my eyes.
     I do not know when I first dreamed that dream,
and cannot now recall how many dreams
have intervened since then. I can't make out
the blurred face of the person in the stern
or if I ever could; he might
be anyone I knew. Maybe he was
still young, had never ridden stern before;
and maybe in the dream—the way dreams can
turn things around to hide the fear
that's hiding underneath another fear—
perhaps I was the one who drowned.
     Only his grasping hand is vivid in my mind,
thrusting above the water's spume,
reaching into the air for me to rescue him—
or if the dream contrived that I
was pictured as the drowning one, the hand

would have to be my hand, and I
would have to see the hand through
someone else's eyes. But I don't know
whom I would choose to be the person there—
someone I loved and who loved me—
to rescue my lone life from inwardness.

     The fact remains that I am still alive,
and I still hope to stay so for a while,
though there are times when I would like
to softly slip away, escape
some overwhelming gloom whose cause
is too diffuse to be identified.
I wonder if it would be worse or better
if I knew; I wonder whether
I do understand what drowning's like,
the numbing chill, the choking gasp,
and whether in that final flash
of consciousness I might be fated
to repeat that same equivocating dream.

     So is that who I am: the mind of doubt
that questions who needs rescuing by whom,
the doubt of who gets rescued in the end,
or if a bloated body is released upon
the undiscriminating shore,
illuminated by a rising moon
among white swirling windswept clouds,
while wafting from the forest mist there floats
an echoed interchange of wailing owls?

At Number Seven

The summer of my freshman college year
I moved back home to New York City where
I hoped to earn some cash and find romance.
My uncle, dashing bachelor that he was,
A second father since my father died,
Would let me drive his red convertible
When I was going on a date; he knew
The windy urgings of desire, but never did
Explain to me why he remained unwed.
    His model Buick was deluxe
As indicated by four simulated
Portholes ostentatiously displayed
Along the fenders on both sides
As if some hierarchy you might
Well imagine was reflected there.
    One Sunday afternoon, as I sped past
The agitated leaves along the road,
A loose-haired girl tight at my side,
I paused at a stop sign that led onto
The highway's open stretch, and as
I waited there another Buick, also red,
Drew next to me. A couple my own age
Were in a car that only had, alas,
Three portholes on its sides, and in a flash
I thrust four rigid fingers in the air
To signal that a race was on
To vindicate my claim of dominance,
And neck-on-neck, we whizzed along
Until my date screamed out at me.

Now skip ahead some thirty years:
You can observe me in a hospital
Recovering from bypass surgery
With tubes of oxygen inside my nose.
An antiseptic nurse wheels a new patient,
Drowsier than I, into the room
To occupy an empty bed.
He tells me he has undergone
A triple bypass, and, without an instant's
Hesitation, I raise up my hand—
Four fingers in fluorescent light
To indicate my bypass was quadruple—
I've excelled in the great universal
Competition to distinguish who I am.

It turned out that the patient was
A rabbi, highly learned, who liked to sermonize;
He lectured that there are accomplishments,
Seven to be exact, that a good life
Needs to include to be complete.
He then enumerated them for me:
A man should love a woman, build a house,
Nurture a child, plant a tree,
Help a good friend, and write a book;
One final thing, the seventh on the list,
He said, you must discover for yourself—
It will reveal the paradox of what
Enables you, at once, to be yourself,
Unique, or anyone at any time.

So skip ahead another thirty years to now;
Listen as I, still troubled, ask myself
What might that seventh item be.
Perhaps the mystery lies in
What the set numbers four and three reveal,
The fact that seven is their sum—

The number promised to disclose what I
Must comprehend to be both me
And anyone. Perhaps those integers
Define a universal ratio as in
A perfect rectangle—a ratio
That does not need my uncle's deluxe car
Or my quadruple surgery
Or any visible accomplishment
To represent itself in time and place.
      Ah yes, a rectangle, a triangle,
A circle, or a square, maybe a star:
All abstract forms that do exist,
And no doubt always have, as an idea,
Impersonal, with no connection to
Some competition I have won or lost.
And, yes, it's true, I'm able to contain
The concept of a ratio within my mind
Without respect to girls or cars
Or rehabilitated hearts, without
A mediating image of myself
Speeding upstate or lying prone in bed.
      That death-denying afternoon
In dusty August when, despite
My unwed uncle-father's wish
To help me seek fulfillment to desire,
I raced to nowhere with the numbers
Four and three, alas, too personal to me—
Not numbers in a ratio beyond
My longing to excel at love. And so
I could not find a self to call my own
That was not merely me, but me transformed
As everyone—as on a seventh day

That I or anyone might understand
To be a holiday within the wind,
A day among illuminated leaves,
One passing day with a girl's blazing hair
Streaming beneath the unobserving sun.

Stories

Long before words were written down—
though we had fire to cook our food—
there lived a hunter and a warrior
who did not like to kill, despite the fact
that his quick hands were good at it. Even
the grouse, the rabbit, and the soft-eyed deer,
whose flesh would feed his family,
pained him to hunt because he knew
no living creature wants to die.
    When his last day arrived, after the year
he lost a daughter from a fever, and a son
who'd wandered off was mangled by
a tusked rampaging boar, he saw himself
defiantly erect before God's throne,
posing the question that he had suppressed
throughout the spinning of his days:
"Why did you make the world this way?" he asked,
"Why do we have to kill in order to
survive? Why is there so much suffering?"
    God whispered His reply: "Stories of war
and violence inspire you humans more
than stories of contentment or of peace—
fathers in grinding conflict with grim sons,
friends greedily betraying friends;
these are the stories you enjoy the most.
Even the sweetness of remorse,
of reconciling love within a family,
are only cherished by you after
everything worth cherishing is lost."

And as he stands transfixed before God's throne,
he knows that God is right about
the whole vast spectacle of suffering—
its power to grip the heart, despite
the counter-yearning to believe prolific life,
when it's unconscious of itself, is able
to achieve some quiet happiness.

In his deep heart he knows true stories
have to end in loss and that unyielding loss
absorbs the mind, its inescapable finality:
he understands shared sorrow is the only
consolation possible for anyone.

He bows his head before this certainty,
then lifts his shaded eyes as they behold
the suffocating dark's descent; he sees
illuminated tears, like distant stars,
flow down God's cheeks, wetting his lips,
before His hand can wipe His tears away.

Sonnetelle of the Dark

I think the darkness changes at the end
With no light left to see the darkness swell—
Darkness that's neither enemy nor friend,
And nothing's left to question or to tell.

This undiscriminating dark without
Relief or variation or the choice
To protest or accept, believe or doubt,
Leaves only hissing silence with a voice.

There won't be even light enough to see
The temporary dark before a flash
Illuminates the branches of a tree—
The consolation of the thunder crash.

This dark knows nothing and it does not care;
This dark does not remember or pretend;
This dark is not aware it's not aware.
This is the changeless darkness at the end.

IV   Laughter

Showing Off in Blue

The IF YOU'VE GOT IT, FLAUNT IT principle
shows Nature in a comic mood
as when, to woo, to win a mate,
the male blue-footed booby struts
his bold arousal in the blaring sun,
flaunting eponymous webbed feet;
he whoops his soaring mating call—
"Thus I implore you to be mine!"—
and joins with lady booby as
their tapered beaks entwine.
        Enticing her with token twigs
as if to start a nest—perhaps a long lost
practice of his ancestors—
now only courtship fills his mind;
a lollapalooza of libidinal display,
his passion overflows the brim,
and I reach out beyond myself
as I identify with him.
        Although my feet are pallid white,
I feel blue when you are not here;
I'm blue when your evasive thoughts
seem to have wandered
somewhere else; and, my beloved,
I am blue with aching apprehension that
my bluest best most eloquent declaiming may
not seem persuasively as true
or heartfelt or appealing as
some hot competitor's brash blue.
        And so I pray my metaphors
of wishful blue—though not

precisely precious as a sapphire
delicately placed upon your throat
of purple-bluish pulsing veins—
will be perceived by you, in making
judgment of my worthiness,
as blues triumphant in their wobbly pains.
      So may the deities of blue,
contriving and inscrutable,
attend and bless me in my
booby-foot ancestral dance
of whoops and stomps and enigmatic sticks,
of choice entwinings, and
the blue uncertainty of chance.

A Toast

There is nothing that has been contrived by man by which
so much happiness is produced as by a good tavern or inn.
—Samuel Johnson

I am enlightened by your claim
that civilization's gift, its power
        to augment human happiness,
is just a tavern or an inn: a mug of beer
        and time to pass the passing hour.

Nothing is unattainable
        if happiness is so defined
as getting woozy in the swell
        of conversation with old friends,
embellishing the self-enhancing tales
        one is inspired to tell.

The trick your modest humor
        shares with all of us
is to constrain desire, relinquish hope
        that happiness can last for long;
we know it can't do that, though
        something in us must believe
sorrow is not our final song.

        Remembering past happiness—
the stroll my love and I
        took to the roiling waterfall
to contemplate its rainbow hues,
        our wandering among red leaves,
made redder in the dappled light
        of yellow tints and liquid blues—

yes, that is sorrowful for being gone,
      forever irretrievable,
not unlike suffering I have endured,
      the death of friends,
for which long mourning brought relief
      as if past sorrow can be cured,

but only for a moment in the mind—
      the mediating mind wherein at last
the sorrow of past happiness
      and happiness of sorrow past
become consoling stories one exchanges
      with companions at an inn:

each boozy tale a quenching elixir,
      a quaff, a mystic brew.
And so, my friend, if I may call you Sam,
      I'll chug-a-lug one down for you!

Parenting Penguins

Since I was a small boy I've wanted to
raise penguins and to own a baby elephant.
Despite my Doctor Doolittle complex,
I knew I did not have the resources—
although our barn had space enough—
to be a mother elephant, but penguins, yes,
that did seem possible to me
throughout my adolescent years
and even into marriage when we had
three human children of our own.
        But when in fleeting time the kids grew up
and left us in the house alone
to live their independent lives,
the thought of penguins popped back
in my mind and seemed to nestle there.
Why not? It's not impossible—what else
would be such fun to do—to romp
with penguins in the lonely afternoons?
Especially I liked the thought
it was the father penguin who
sat on the egg and incubated it,
keeping it safe from harm, keeping it warm
while resting on its father's feet
beneath a special flap of skin.
        I wrote to tell my son about
the plans I was considering,
but he assumed some gentle teasing
would be his appropriate response,
and so he did some research on the needs
of penguins under human care.

Since they are social animals,
he tactfully replied, the minimum
I'd have to take into my care was ten,
and twenty would be better still;
I'd have to build a pool that was
at least fifteen feet at the deepest end;
supplying fish for them would cost me
several thousand bucks a year;
and, finally, the crushing detail that
weakened my resolution to proceed:
someone would have to be assigned to feed
the penguins six or seven times a day.
     "No way will I feed twenty penguins
seven times a day!" my wife proclaimed.
"We have six cats and that's enough;
including you, that's seven mouths to feed."
But on our anniversary my wife
presented me with twenty penguins
and an elephant, their bellies plump with cotton,
all approving me with rolling eyes.
     And so that ended it, and so
I wrote back to my expert son—
expositor of penguin happiness—
to thank him for the research he had done.
No further fantasy of parenting
to build on there. I can't erase
the picture of tame penguins frolicking
from my adjusted mind,
but I've concluded, even though
our children are dispersed across the continent,
I'd better stick to human fathering.

Skunk Family

Welcome! Welcome! Mr. and Mrs. Skunk,
I'm pleased to have you make your nest
below our overhanging deck
and raise your brood so I can watch
all eight of you parade into our flower bed,
then cross our lawn and disappear
into the deeper grass to forage after
bugs and grasshoppers. Bon appétit!
    We have no special use for the crawl space
beneath our house, so why not use it to
accommodate a family like yours!
I still can hear my mother lecture me
across the years from when I was a boy:
"Bobby, you've got to learn to share,
you've got to learn risk goes with trust,"
and I am sure that she'd be proud of me,
proud that I took to heart her teaching
and concern for others needs, necessities.
    I must take care I'm not too nosey in
observing you, respected guests; there is
a limit as to how close we can get
in understanding what a stranger
understands—that in exchange for living
under our house entirely rent free,
you let us watch you poke around and play
and make a show of how a family
naturally is organized so we can add
our human specialties—awareness,
and approval, and delight—as when
one disobeying skunkling wanders off

and Mom comes after him and grabs him by
his shiny scruff and brings him back to join
his brothers and his sisters and his dad.
That's discipline, and families thrive best
when innate unity has been preserved—
as often my own mom reminded me.
　　　Now evening shadows settle in
the shrubs and bushes that surround our house—
the airy house that our invention built,
the house we have agreed to share;
a sleepy wind arises from the stream,
and from the swelling honeysuckle
wafts its sweet aroma everywhere.

Accident in Red

Prepared for when she visited, we kept
a giant box of crayons in our house.
Her concentration when she drew
was so intense it seemed to send out waves
that we could feel, and so as grandparents
we thought that we were right to be concerned.
   She rarely drew forms we could recognize,
though images like sun or moon or stars
appeared along the margins of the paper
we provided her. But in the center there
would always be just zigzag lines or swirls
and colors piled in layers on themselves.
   I well recall the ice storm with cracked branches
snapping from their stems on the wild day
she drew exclusively in swirling reds
with neither sun nor moon nor pointed stars
to frame unnamable and twisted shapes.
I asked her what her drawing was about,
attempting to sound casual, but she—
I still can hear her thin voice now—replied:
"Three elephants have had an accident."
   A faint smile curled her tightened lips
as if she were reluctant to express
what must have been amusement at
deflecting of adult pretentiousness.
In her mind, I surmised, her drawing didn't
need to have a subject other than itself.
   So you can see, my thoughts confronting her
got tangled as they tried to penetrate
her thoughts, though, as I said, we had been right

to worry if some danger threatened her.
One might still speculate that red has been
the color that defined the choices she
has made throughout her swirling life, despite
brief visitations of the sun or moon
that she could share with us or anyone.

    And yet, the more the spinning years go by
so evanescent and unchronicled,
the funnier her answer sounds to me—
funny in its intentional red sense—
and accurate for anyone who is
concerned with elephants and accidents.

Anticipating Paradise

The secret source of Humor is not joy but sorrow.
There is no humor in heaven. — Mark Twain

What if I come upon an angel
snoozing on a grassy riverbank,
and at a whim I slide beside him
(maybe her—it's hard to tell)
and poke my fingers in his ribs
to tickle him just for the fun of it!
    If Twain is right in what he claims,
the drowsy angel will not laugh.
Would he (or she) assume
that my attempt at making friends
lacked well-bred reticence?
    And what if I, a newcomer,
not yet attuned to heaven's rules,
recall some sorrow from my life—
betrayal or rejection or neglect—
too painful still for sweet oblivion
and thus requiring music
for relief? If heaven does
provide an orchestra, must it,
serenely humorless, exclude
the babble of bassoons,
the giggle of paired piccolos?
    Perhaps for visitors like me,
bemused and skeptical, a course
(with manual) is offered that provides
advice and information as to how
one should prepare for permanence,
for marriage inexhaustible
with new positions and techniques,
the long haul of eternity.

And if, as an experiment,
I tried to tell the Lord a joke—
say, Groucho's famous joke
about not wanting to become
a member of a club that would
accept the likes of him—
would He, although omniscient, still
be puzzled by the fact
He missed the innuendo
of my anecdote, and flustered thus
request that I explain myself—
a smart-ass self, I must confess,
a self that takes pride
in its bottomless humility.
    O Heaven and ah woeful earth—
NEVER THE TWAIN SHALL MEET!
and thus for unrepentant me,
a literary marksman and
elect of all the non-elect,
puntificator with forked tongue,
no doubt I'd be cast out for good,
yet not without some consolation since
the punishment I'm surely worthy of
would just be to abide—gee whiz!—
a little pungent while right here,
a little longer where the laughter is.

Tickling

Like human children, chimpanzee babies
Also are ticklish. They'll flail about
As if they're swimming through the air;
Whatever purpose this response fulfills,
Improving muscles to increase their powers
To survive—like learning how to laugh,
It's in their genes as it's in ours.
   And it's peculiar that we can't
Achieve the same effect if we should try
Ticking ourselves; our bodies, all alone,
Are not sufficient to assuage their needs.
To hold back gloom, fancy requires new laws
To overcome the grimness of desire,
Transforming giggles to guffaws.

Worms

I've been on medication for
high blood pressure throughout my adult life,
the same disease my father suffered from.
I'm used to a routine of popping pills,
but one day, staring at the pristine sky,
as dreamily I gulped them down,
my wife cried out: "For God's sake, Bob,
you've taken pills intended to
prevent our dogs from getting worms—
heartworms that can cause death;
they're powerful, they're dangerous,
they are not meant for human hearts!"
But I did not get sick, not even
dizziness or nausea afflicted me,
though one might think the reason I
did not get worms was really due
to my imbibing pills meant for big dogs.
My health remained exactly as it was,
so all in all, I thought, my prospects
in this world were looking up.
Yet maybe taking heartworm pills
was my half-conscious way of blocking out
the truth that worms devour us in the end;
confusing heartworm pills with those
for blood pressure perhaps expressed
some rebel wish to circumvent my fate,
or maybe, so I claimed, I was just trying
for a heartfelt laugh to entertain my wife.

Darwin, embracing parent of us all,
loved worms and thought of them as gardeners
who plowed the land before our ancestors
invented plows, and they could then succeed
as farmers only with the help of worms
enabling roots to penetrate the ground,
enabling all varieties of seedlings to
take hold, secure themselves, and flourish there.
   And thus Darwin instructed me
to look down to the earth where now
I can behold prodigious diggers who
inhabit their own paradise of touch,
of wet and dry, of soft and hard; dwelling
contentedly in unrushed time, they bury
to renew, digest in order to restore.
   Underground angels, never ceasing in
essential work of nitrifying
bones of animals, shells of insects,
twigs, and leaves; protectors of
our mundane health, our vigor to survive
if only for a heartfelt while;
adorers of restorative decay,
keep our fields fertile, our land green—to you
I sing out hallelujah and hoorah!

Jasper

Concealed in the lush flower garden as
an evening storm comes on, hunting perhaps
or only passing time, Jasper, so I assume,
is thinking thoughts that cautious cats
have immemorially thought.

My wife, preparing soup, steps out
the kitchen door to summon him;
uncertain for an instant, Jasper
considers if it is beneath
his dignity to come when called.

He pauses at her feet, goes limp, so she
can lift him up and bring him in the house.
"Good Jasper boy," she says, and I assume
he understands. But she's not finished
with her accolades: "Handsome fellow,
your ancestors were surely kings"
augments her praise, which he acknowledges
by leaping on the counter for his meal,
then, satisfied, he settles in a chair,
his favorite, dreaming no doubt what cats
have immemorially dreamed.

And I can only guess what thoughts
float through my wife's reclusive mind
as she returns to slicing celery and carrots
for her secret recipe. "More pepper"
might be all the conscious words she needs,
though maybe some uncertain thoughts
with no connection to preparing soup—
thoughts of our distant daughter's
inconclusive diagnoses—darkens

an underlying mood, a shadow mood
of which perhaps she dimly is aware.

All this, of course, is just my guess
which may have no relationship to her,
revealing only something about me,
and yet what might connect observing
Jasper emerging from his hiding place,
and what I think my wife might possibly
be thinking now, is galaxies beyond
what reasoned words can comprehend.

Jasper wakes up and looks at me;
I think he thinks there may be something
on my mind that might pertain to him;
his body stiffens as he fixes on
some rustling sound outside the door.
I tell my wife, "A cat will bristle
at the slightest shift of wind," but she replies that
"Something recently has worried him;
perhaps he picks the worry up from you."

Can that be true? Can she intuit
something about me just by watching Jasper
scamper from his chair? Or am I able
to detect what might be troubling her
by what she seems to have observed
in how Jasper and I respond to what
each thinks is on the other's mind?
Perhaps the singular connection here
is that we hear the same wind at the door
or else the barking of our neighbor's dogs
whom Jasper, a survivor, outmaneuvers
with his many lives—a Jewish cat,
so let his enemies take note.

My wife adds pepper to the soup—
a careful sprinkle, nothing more, tastes it
and, yes, she's satisfied, as I will be

come dinnertime, and Jasper, sleeping
in the chair that recollects his shape,
also will be satisfied, and everywhere on earth
each household cat, survivors all,
content in its own mystery, gives aid
and consolation to the wives and husbands
who depend on them to fill the silences
where words can't reach, to fill them,
and, beyond uncertainties, be satisfied.

Panegyric for Charles Darwin's Nose

for John Glendening

Before Captain Fitz-Roy began
His five-year journey on the Beagle
To explore the coast of South America,
He interviewed Charles Darwin whom
He thought to be God-fearing, pious,
And thus suitable to share his cabin
And to dine with him when he was not
Exceedingly morose—although
He ended up by taking his own life.
      But Fitz-Roy didn't like the young man's nose,
Believing that a man's true character
Revealed itself according to
The contours of his face. Despite
His reservations, Fitz-Roy asked Darwin
To enlist as the ship's naturalist
To study new terrains, new habitats.
Despite his father's fervent hopes
That Charles would serve the holy church,
He gave his son consent to go.
      Consider, wide-eyed reader, this
Incredible contingency! Had Fitz-Roy chosen
Someone else because he didn't like
The twist of Darwin's nose which showed,
So Fitz-Roy thought, a lack of energy,
The history of science might have followed
Quite a different path in understanding
Why we have emerged to be the creatures
That we are: cruel and competing,
Struggling with others and, because

We're also capable of sympathy,
Struggling as well with our split selves.

Just random chance, contingency,
Something sublimely trivial—the shape
Of Darwin's nose—that almost did,
But didn't quite, sufficiently offend
Fitz-Roy's exquisite sensibility,
Turned the fortuitous into our fate
To comprehend contingency itself,
What well might cause our warring species
To destroy itself or to survive perhaps
Through some emergent self-control.

Darwin's wife, Emma, married him for love,
Not only to pass on her genes, although
She bore ten children; little Annie died
Of fever when she was just ten years old;
Another died of who knows what in infancy.
Emma, however, kept her faith and thought
That God created all the animals
As they are now, six thousand years ago;
He fashioned humankind in His own image,
But justly banished our first parents
From protected Eden when they disobeyed
His clear commands for self-restraint.
Emma believed that Jesus was
The needed savior of us all; it deeply
Troubled her that Charles had doubts.

So here's the nitty-gritty choice
That Darwin had to make: whether the world,
As he'd been brought up to assume,
Was made by God, with moral laws to guide
Our wayward impulses—or else
Did we evolve through adaptation,
Struggle, and raw randomness,
From variation, he so carefully observed,

As in the size of finches' beaks,
With no hope of transcending death.

     Contingency! Contingency is what we find
Who seek some consolation for mere accident,
For suffering, for knowledge
Even species won't survive. Just understanding
Is what Darwin's gloomy theory offers us:
Blind variation and descent
Wins the debate, but only by a nose,
And earns our admiration for his courage
To reject the soothing fables of the past.

     And so I picture him and laugh out loud,
His awkward nose advancing into fame
And notoriety. O nose extravagant,
O nose unique, inquiring nose,
Nose of discovery, of revelation
And astonishment, I offer praise to thee!
Enraptured connoisseur of beetles and
Old tell-tale bones, Darwin, I see you still
Astride a giant long-lived tortoise on
The rocky shore of the Galápagos,
Your nose held high into the tropic light.

Worrying

My mother was not superstitious, though
When she felt glum, she would allow herself
To wish she could believe in paradise—
Not a vague afterlife of disembodied souls
Devoid of faces that can smile or frown,
But a bright place where one enjoyed good food.
      And yet a part of her might be
Called mystical—her certitude
That worrying could mitigate or change,
If not the fate of nations or societies,
At least what happened to her loved ones as
They tried to make sense of their lives.
      I still recall the day she phoned, a tremble
In her voice, to tell me that my sister's son,
The family's adventurer, informed her that
He planned to spend a year in Africa
To learn what other cultures celebrate
And how they manage to survive.
      My mom's first worrying response was what,
For God's sake, would he have to eat;
Could he endure under conditions that
He'd never seen or known before?
      "But where in Africa will he reside?"
Was my bemused reply. "Africa's huge—
A continent from sea to sea like ours.
The countries there are not the same,
Not all are dangerous; he'll be all right."
      My mother paused to meditate upon
The possibilities now challenging

Her power to be effectively concerned.
And then the thought exploded from her lips:
"Zabar's! That's where he'll spend the year."

   The slight dyslexia that runs throughout
Our family had served her well:
She felt a momentary calm. Zabar's,
Only a minor verbal variation from
Zimbabwe or Zaire, sounded
Familiar, manageable, safe to her.

   And yet, how could a skeptic like myself
Respond except by telling her what she
Already knew from actual experience:
Zabar's is multicultural New York's
Most bountiful Jewish delicatessen,
World-famous for its cornucopia
Of true gourmet delights: smoked salmon,
Bagels, chicken soup with matzo balls,
Kosher pastrami, corned beef, juicy franks,
Küchen to satisfy the sweetest tooth.

   If there's a Zabar's somewhere in
The tangles of remotest Africa,
I teased my mom, she wouldn't have
To worry her beloved grandson
Might not have sufficient nourishment.
But she was not assuaged; some deeper fear,
Something that still eluded her, required
Her worrying. And I soon realized that I
Was wrong to minimize her need to feel
Her worrying was helpful in this world.

   And if I were to fantasize that she
Could journey back for just a day, I'd ask
If she is happy in the afterlife:
"Is there a Zabar's somewhere in the clouds
Where you can have your breakfast now

Of salmon, cream cheese, küchen, tea,
Without your worrying about the children
Of the world, including Africa,
Whether they're cared for as they need to be—
Whether they have nutritious food to eat?"

Exchanging Names

My mother sometimes called me by
My father's name long after he had died;
Sometimes she called her brother by
My name or called me by her brother's name
Or called her grandsons interchangeably,
All three of them, each by each other's name
Until she got it right on second try.

My father on his deathbed—so Mother
Informed me when the time had come
To choose what college to attend—
Picked Dartmouth as the perfect school.
Though she could not recall the reasons why,
Yet she was sure that was his final wish,
What he determined would be best for me.
His certainty left nothing to discuss,
And I departed with Mom's blessings on
One luminous September day.

But in my sophomore year, vaguely
Dissatisfied, I told my mother that
I wanted to change schools and attend
Columbia back in New York, the city
That I knew from childhood on. Maybe
I missed the crowds, the anonymity,
The flashing company of girls
(Dartmouth had not yet gone coed),
Or maybe what I felt was just
Inevitable homesickness.

My unconvincing explanation was
Most Dartmouth students didn't like
Discussing books, and yet I felt serene

Observing the impartial sparkle of
The country sky or on the silent walks
I took along the nearby river as the ice
Receded and the maples bared red buds
In promise of oncoming spring.

But she was adamant: my father's wish
Decreed that Dartmouth was my destiny,
That I was meant to graduate from there.
"Don't you have teachers you admire to whom
You've grown attached?" my mother asked.

And so at Dartmouth I remained, and so
I walked along that frozen river in
Constricted winter or in thawing spring,
Or looked up in the clear pulsating night
To see what constellations I had learned
To recognize and to identify.

Five years flowed by, or maybe more;
Some details fade and cannot be recalled
With certainty. Again we're having lunch,
Which has become our monthly ritual,
When from the shadow of her frown,
My mother blurts out that she still
Feels guilty for not letting me
Change colleges: "Surely your father
Would have understood," she pleads.

Now skip ahead another dozen years:
We're sitting at a crowded street café
With gourds and spices hanging from the beams,
And I can recognize my mother's frown,
The twisted way her smile descends,
As she confesses that she still regrets
Preventing me from changing schools:
"I fear I might have done some harm,"
She says, "I think you could be happier."

"What's gone is gone and can't be changed"
Was how I groped to comfort her.
And yet her shaken thoughts come spilling forth:
"There's something that I never could admit,"
She says, "I'm not sure Dartmouth was the school
Your father named with his last breath;
Williams was what he might have said."

    My first reaction was appalled dismay;
I wondered if I might have followed
Quite a different path: might I have married
Someone else and had just daughters who all lived
Not far away from me, or maybe had a son
Who joined the army with a purpose that
Befitted him, or joined a business firm,
Made money, got elected governor?
From what abyss did such thoughts come
That never occupied my settled mind
In those cascading years preceding when
I found myself astonished on that day
My mother's secret was revealed?

    But then my body started in to laugh
With sobs and spasms shaking to my bones—
As if such laughter had been lurking there.
My mother was confused what in this world
I possibly could have been laughing at;
She called me by father's name, then mine,
And then joined in despite herself—"Williams!"
The unwilled name leapt wildly from her lips.

    The life I never lived, can never know,
No longer beckons me; accepting laughter,
Echoing throughout the star-strewn universe,
Appears as power that can send me on my way,
And that must mean I'm on my own at last—
Or so my mother said at lunch today.

An Elephant by Aristotle

Elephants also need to dream,
And when one suffers from insomnia,
So Aristotle wrote in his vast work
"On Animals," painstakingly described,
The cure that will restore him to good health
Can be effected if his shoulders are
"rubbed with warm water, olive oil, and salt."
In his discerning study of the animals,
Amphibians and fish, insects and birds,
Describing how their organs serve their needs,
He claimed the legendary elephant
Exceeded other creatures with "its wit
And its intelligence," though what he meant
By wit is open to our speculation still.
        I recently had graduated from
An elite college where I learned all this
And much more that I didn't know—
Delightful as such knowledge was—
How to apply it to my life. Depressed,
I was uncertain whether I should be
A doctor or a lawyer or just make
A lot of money as my uncle had.
        My roommate's family lived on a farm;
They had an empty barn with stalls
That weren't being used. And so I thought,
Before I could collect myself and make
The consequential choice of a career,
I would, still single, unattached,
Indulge myself and thus acquire
A baby elephant, since Aristotle had

Assured me, "They are easy tempered and
Domesticated easily."
My plan was that I'd keep him in the barn
All languid summer long, and in the fall
I'd sell him to the zoo up in the Bronx
With an agreement that I'd have
The right to visit him at leisure on
Slow weekends and on holidays.

    I need to warn you that this favorite
Remembrance only has begun: unlikely
As it sounds, an ad from Bloomingdale's
Appeared in the bland *New York Times*
Announcing that they'd purchased, and would give
To some deserving zoo, a baby elephant
Whose mother had been shot and killed—
No doubt by hunters poaching ivory—
Just like the elephant of my imagining,
The one I'd always wanted to adopt.

    You need to know we get names wrong
In our dyslexic family, and I called Macy's
By mistake, but when they transferred me
To an impatient salesman in
Their stocked department of stuffed toys,
I realized my error and hung up the phone.
And when I next called Bloomingdale's,
The manager inquired what zoo
I represented and expressed contempt
When I explained quite simply that
My motive was my love of elephants:
Was that too hard for him to understand?

    I had to borrow money, piles of it,
To cover the outrageous asking price,
From my bemused and wealthy uncle with
A bachelor's flair for wild extravagance,
And I was able, you'll be pleased to know,

To outbid the astounded New York zoos
With their tight budgets and constraints.
　　　All summer long my elephant and I
Cavorted in the purple clover field
Or splashed each other in the lily pond;
Ears still, he'd sneak up from behind
And put his trunk between my legs,
Lift up, and tumble me head forward
In the cartwheel spin I had to learn
To play my part in our invented game.
This well might be considered wit, "panting
A sound just like a sighing man," as Aristotle
Had foreseen so many books ago.
　　　So, Aristotle, thanks to you I knew
Just how to rub the shoulders of
My parabolic pachyderm
With the prescribed ingredients
To spare him from such dreams as cause
Insomnia, dread falling dreams of loneliness,
Bereavement, or abandonment.
My laughing gratitude calls out to you,
Dear founding father of philosophy,
Observer with an eye for wonder and
Astonishment, for how detail and fact
And information, tempered with, ah yes!
A touch of delicate embellishment,
Can be recalled to rescue us from gloom
And flourish forth some waking happiness.

Identity

Driving home late at night after
reading from my new book of poems
at Valley University, I was pulled over by a cop
who claimed that I was speeding in
a slow-down zone. He asked to see
my registration, but I couldn't find it
in the glove compartment, nor
had I remembered to include
my driver's license with my credit card.

"How do I know you are who you
now claim to be? You could be anyone,
and this could be a stolen car," the cop,
not without reason, challenged me.
"I have no choice but to arrest you,
and you'll have to spend the night in jail
until someone who really knows
your true identity can bail you out."

But ah! inspired, here's what I then
proposed to him: "Look, officer," said I,
"here is a copy of my newest book;
just turn to any page, give me the title
of the poem, and I'll recite it for you
so you'll know I am the person that
I claim to be." I handed him the book;
he opened to a random page, gave me
the title of a poem, and I recited it to him
with all the gusto I could muster
with just him as my attending audience.

He leaned in closer and perused my face,
and I took out my pen and autographed

the book for him and stuck it out
the window as a plea and as a gift,
but he refused it, scolding me:
"I don't read bullshit, only facts;
I don't like it when people make things up
or say things in a fancy way.
So take this as a warning now—go home
tell this true story to your wife,
assuming that you've really got a wife;
you don't look like the kind of guy
who might learn something from a night in jail,
though you were speeding; that's a fact."
        At first I was relieved to be let off,
and yet it rankled me that he was not
moved by the poem I read—a poem
about a man and woman strolling though
the winter woods, fresh snow upon the trees,
a wary squirrel watching them—
a sight that he, too, might enjoy,
assuming that he had a wife;
and, even more, it bothered me, perverse
as this may seem, that he perceived me as
incapable of learning from
just punishment. He got me wrong,
completely wrong, that is not who I am!
        I almost turned my car around
to seek him out and tell him that I'm not
afraid of jail—it might bring forth a poem—
and I will speed again if I think that
by chance I'd get away with it. Ah yes,
I'll sit him down, and standing over him,
whoever he might be beneath his uniform,
I'll make him listen to my whole damn book!

Glockenspiel

But as passions, whether violent or not, must never be expressed
in such a way as to excite disgust, and as music, even in the most
terrible situations, must never offend the ear, but please the
hearer, or in other words must never cease to be music.
— A letter from Mozart to his father

The last thing I remember saying as
they wheeled me down the sterile corridor,
transported to the operating room,
was "Doctor, don't forget the heart is not
merely an organ, it also is a metaphor;
it has a musical, iambic beat."
"No wonder it's so sturdy," he replied.

The anesthesiologist, who needed
some persuasion, had agreed to strap
my earphones on me just as I
was coming back to consciousness
when in the limbo of recovery
so I could listen to *The Magic Flute*,
my choice to represent how lilting art,
enhancing transient life, transfigures us.

My reasoning was that whatever world
I found myself inhabiting would be
desirable if Mozart's opera,
transcending ugliness and violence,
laughter's perfected complement,
could find its home and flourish there.

When I awoke I found myself
inside an entryway where Mozart
welcomed me as if we were old friends:
"You're just in time for a rehearsal of
Die Zauberflöte!" he exclaimed.
"We're at the moment late in the first act

when Papageno, lusty bird-catcher—
with whom you always have identified—
calls to his magic bells to rescue him,
"komm, du schönes glockenspiel" and charms cruel
Monostatos and his attendant slaves
who would imprison him. But now, entranced
by his bright chimes, his adversaries start
a stately dance, singing in unison,
"Das klinget so herrlich, das klinget so schön,"
as words become celebratory sounds.

He handed me the resonating bells,
and to my stunned astonishment,
I played them perfectly as if I'd trained
to take part in an orchestra like this
throughout my earthbound life, as if to make
such joyful music is the purpose that
suffering life aspires to and requires:
music mellifluous, marvelous music that
has power to free one from oneself into
impersonal yet mellow happiness.

But that is not the final time
that Papageno needs his glockenspiel.
When in despair that he won't find a wife,
about to hang himself upon a tree, three boys,
who represent his fundamental innocence,
like Shakespeare's Ariel, appear at once,
and they remind him of his magic bells
that he so foolishly forgot: "Ich Narr!
vergass der zauberdinge," he cries out
as he begins to play. And conjured by
the tolling of these tones, his wished-for wife,
the fertile Papagena, now transformed
from eighty back to eighteen years of age,
appears and eagerly embraces him.

When I awoke again and my true wife,
who'd waited silent through the silent night,
was there to greet me, asking how I felt,
I answered her—or else whatever spirit
was emboldened and attuned who now
had potency to speak through me—
declaiming "Klinget, Glöckchen, Klinget," my
own minor inspiration to amuse,
to send out laughter through the universe.
And yet my wife would have the final say,
telling the doctor with his fingers on my pulse:
"I know him, doctor, he will be okay!"

V   Epilogue

Genie

for Marcus Klein

A longtime pessimist, having observed
firsthand the vanity of human
aspirations and desires, Rabbi Ezekiel,
now old and burdened with regrets,
"a daughter married to a lazy schlub,
a son in faraway America,"
surveyed the Mediterranean shore
of ancient embarkations and retreats.
Searching the beach for spiraled shells
as fragile souvenirs of transient life,
he stubbed his toe on a blue bottle
almost hidden underneath the sand.

He brushed the grit off of its sides,
and LO! out popped a genie with white curls,
a shiny yarmulke upon his head.
"Don't stare at me like that!" the genie
reprimanded him, "why shouldn't Jews
have Jewish genies to attend their needs?"

"It's usual to get three wishes,"
he declared, "according to the formula,
but you're not looking at a genie of
high rank; all I can offer you is just
one wish, so make your choice judiciously."

A pious thought occurred to glum Ezekiel—
that he might make a wish to ease
the struggle underneath our common sun
of animals and humans, all alike
in needing food and being doomed to die.
Surely the genie would approve
this altruistic sentiment. "I'll wish,"

he murmured, "for a universal peace
to end all forms of prejudice."
    The genie slapped his head, knocking
his yarmulke askew. "Oye veh!" he cried,
"that isn't possible. By nature Nature
preys upon itself; after the flood
Yahweh revised the rules so Noah could
devour red meat as well as plants,
despite the dread that caused the animals—
see chapter nine of Genesis.
You'll have to improvise another wish."
    Ezekiel thought hard and the idea
leapt to his mind that if he can't assuage
some suffering afflicting humankind,
maybe he still might aid his fellow Jews.
And so he wished that oil be found right there
on that stark shore where they now stood—
oil would help Israel's economy.
"That's a humungous wish for me to grant—
a worn-out genie who is making do
with worn-out powers. Try again,
but stick to something personal
like winning the town lottery, or else
relief for that arthritis in your back.
Don't keep your private feelings bottled up,"
the genie added, pleased with his own quip.
    "I must confess," Ezekiel replied,
"I've been denied much pleasure in my life,
serving my congregation, following
the strictures of our holy book.
Here is a recent photo of my wife—
she ain't what you'd call beautiful.
Can't you improve her looks a little bit,
make her a little thinner, sexier,
to warm the chill of my declining age?"

The genie stared at the creased picture of
the rabbi's wife: after a pause—drawn out
and hanging heavy in the air—he said,
"Let's see if oil can be discovered here;
for sure, we'll have to count on lady luck."
    A month goes by, and once again
Ezekiel is wandering along
the hieroglyphic beach, observing foam
that bubbles its insistent syllables,
and it amuses him to conjure up
a scene in which his genie finds a bottle
almost buried in the sand, rubs it, and LO!
another genie pops out with a flourish
of his velvet shawl. The rabbi likes
the logic that wish-granting genies must
depend on other genies who can grant
their wishes if acknowledged as their own.
    And with this floating fantasy in mind—
of genies bringing forth more genies
multiplying on into infinity—
Ezekiel knows that though he'd like to be
a high-ranked genie with the power to
alleviate the sorrows of the world,
at least those sorrows caused by us,
by granting wishes that reside within
the rounded realm of possibility,
he'll have to be content at last just telling
genie jokes to strangers, making friends
whose laughter frolics in the lilting foam.